Creative Novel Writing

CREATIVE
NOVEL WRITING

ROSELLE ANGWIN

ROBERT HALE · LONDON

© *Roselle Angwin 1999*
First published in Great Britain 1999

ISBN 0 7090 6344 X

Robert Hale Limited
Clerkenwell House
Clerkenwell Green
London EC1R 0HT

The right of Roselle Angwin to be identified as
author of this work has been asserted by her
in accordance with the Copyright, Designs and
Patents Act 1988.

2 4 6 8 10 9 7 5 3 1

Typeset in North Wales by
Derek Doyle & Associates, Mold, Flintshire.
Printed in Great Britain by
St Edmundsbury Press Limited, Bury St Edmunds
and bound by
WBC Book Manufacturers Limited, Bridgend.

This book is offered with love and thanks to all those who made it through to the end of the Novel course in Plymouth through the winter of 1997/8, without whom it would not have been possible.

Acknowledgements

Acknowledgement is made for passages quoted in the text:

Extracts by permission of Fourth Estate Ltd from *The Shipping News* by E. Annie Proulx © 1993 by E. Annie Proulx.

Extracts of approximately 345 words from pp.90–1 and 127 from *As I Walked Out One Midsummer Morning* by Laurie Lee (Penguin Books, 1971) copyright © Laurie Lee, 1969. Reproduced by permission of Penguin Books Ltd.

The author and publisher would also like to acknowledge other books quoted in the text: *The Way to Write*, by John Moat and John Fairfax (Elm Tree Books 1981), lines from the Introduction by Ted Hughes; *Inner Work* by Robert Johnson (Harper & Row 1989); *The Horse Whisperer*, by Nicholas Evans (Bantam Press 1995, Corgi 1996); *Separation*, by Dan Franck (Editions du Seuil, Paris, 1991, Black Swan 1995); *The English Patient* by Michael Ondaatje (Bloomsbury 1992, Picador 1993); *Aspects of the Novel*, by E.M. Forster (Edward Arnold 1927, Penguin 1990).

Gratitude is due to the inspiration that has also come from lectures at Dartington by Lindsay Clarke and Ben Okri, and their books.

The author would particularly like to thank the participants who brought such enthusiasm, generosity and commitment to her course 'A Novel in Two Terms', out of which grew this book; and also Jeannie Arbuckle, Lyn Browne and Chris Tooke for their permission to use extracts from workshop exercises.

Contents

Introduction

Storytelling goes back, as far as we can tell, to the beginnings of human life on this planet. Storytellers are keepers of wisdom; they weave spells which feed the human soul. In Old Welsh, the same word is used for both storytelling and instruction or guidance. The storyteller was a seer.

The novelist, of course, is carrying on this tradition, albeit through the written rather than the spoken word. If you have chosen to write a novel, it is presumably because you feel you have a story worth telling. The purpose of this book is to enable you to find the most imaginative and effective way to express it.

Perhaps it's important, as writers, to ask both why we write, and why we read. The most obvious answer to the latter, of course, is to do with entertainment, amusement, even escapism – to pass the time. But reading also has a deeper purpose, to do with increasing our knowledge of the world and of ourselves. We read to learn, to inform ourselves, to expand our understanding and awareness, to reassure ourselves that we are not alone, to make sense of the world and to see 'how other people do it'. Books give us glimpses, as E.M. Forster remarked, into secret lives.

Reading can also perform the function of healing. Common to every human is the search for belonging, for love, meaning, truth, fulfilment and joy; we all share fears of suffering and death, loneliness, lovelessness and meaninglessness. One of the most fundamental functions of writing as well as reading is to explore, whether in fictional or non-fictional form, some of these issues. Lawrence

Durrell reputedly once suggested that a writer passes a current along a wire, and in so doing frees him- or herself as well as others from doubts and terrors.

An author needs to bear all these possible purposes of literature in mind; a book, no matter how riveting, how wise, will only be as good as its ability to hold the reader's attention, to communicate.

Writers, in a way, straddle the borderlands of the inner world of the imagination and the outer world of experience. If they are able to bring the two together, their creative efforts will not only entertain the reader, but may also have the capacity to uplift, enlighten and transform. Words can change lives.

Once upon a time, art of all kinds was seen as central to the health of both the individual and the culture in which he or she lived. There is undoubtedly a connection between the imagination, and its expression or exercise, and optimum psychological health. 'To awaken the pictures that live in our story-imagination is to become more radiantly and fully alive,' says Nancy Mellon in *Storytelling and the Art of the Imagination*. Native Americans would say that stories are powerful medicine; stories can restore a sense of wellbeing in the listener or reader in a way that little else can. It's no coincidence that some of our myths are hundreds and even thousands of years old. 'Inherent in story is the power to reorder a state of psychological confusion,' says travel writer and essayist Barry Lopez. 'The stories had renewed in me a sense of the purpose of life. This feeling, an inexplicable renewal of enthusiasm after storytelling, is familiar to many people.'

I am, of course, not the first person to remark that we live in strange times. Our society tends to value information, technology and rationality over wisdom, feeling and imagination. Our bias for the last few hundred years has been towards what is known in some circles as the 'left brain' – that is, towards thinking that is rooted in logic, linear processes, analytical understanding and codification. The 'right-brain' values of intuition, imagination, feeling, image-based thought processes and a lateral approach have not been accorded much room or credence. Another way of expressing left and right brain is conscious mind versus unconscious mind. The unconscious part of ourselves is the part that in the past was valued through attention to dream, vision, ritual and religious experience. This is where memories, feelings and imagination abide, and inform the artistic process. This is where stories originate, too. Creative writing is a way of keeping the channels open between this hidden part of ourselves and the conscious mind; good fiction, like good poetry, can open these channels for other people, too, into the rich world of the imagination. A story is like an Ariadne's thread. I've witnessed the power of this over and over in workshops.

Inspired writing which not only makes sense to the head but also comes from and speaks to the heart is a joy both to produce and to read. Writers, I believe, use both the left and right brain if they are writing well. Neither, of course, is complete without the other; both functions need to work in harmony. Your success as a novelist may be rooted in your ability to create original and exciting language – which so often is based on feeling and imagery – but will still depend on finding the appropriate shape for your imaginings. Inspiration and imagination need a structure, a form, if they are to communicate. Your job as a writer is to open the channels, the doors, between the unconscious and the conscious mind, in yourself and for your readers. 'Storytelling,' says Whitbread prizewinner Lindsay Clarke, 'opens a passage from feeling to meaning, converting raw matter to order.'

As a writer and creative writing tutor, I am continually astonished and excited by the power of the imagination. I am constantly looking for new ways of accessing and supporting the creative process and enabling imaginative writing. My background in psychology also reminds me daily of the potency of the unconscious mind and its ability to offer inspiration and wisdom. Over the years in which I have been facilitating workshops I have developed a number of strategies for stimulating creativity in writing. This book combines these with notes for a twenty-week novel-writing course I have been tutoring. It is intended to be a practical book, and intersperses general exercises designed to stimulate the imagination with specific workshop guidelines for writing a novel.

I don't know if creative writing can be taught. Certainly the techniques can be learnt, but the inspirational process itself depends on a number of factors, some of which are unquantifiable (which is appropriate for a right-brain function). There are, however, many ways of enabling the creative process, or at least creating the conditions in which it may take root and bloom. Something happens – factor X – at the point where technique and imagination meet; a kind of alchemy. It's as if the two realms of conscious technique and unconscious imagery meet and create a volatile seam which may suddenly erupt into fire, like flames flaring along a petrol trail.

There are a number of good books available which focus on writing techniques. My aim is not to swell these numbers, but instead to attempt to find ways to redress the balance of which I've been speaking; to help create the conditions for an alchemical encounter to take place. Clearly, the novel-writing core of this book requires an amount of exploration of form and structure. My interest, though, as you will probably have gathered, is in exploring how we can create exciting, impassioned, authentic, vivid language which sings and sparkles and communicates its story effectively.

As readers, we require that a book leaves us in some way changed; if it doesn't, it has perhaps not fulfilled its potential. I hope, in this attempt, to help – if only in a minor way – keep the candles of imagination and inspiration burning in any of you writers who are looking for the most powerful way to communicate your vision to the world. At the very least, I'd like to think that working your way through this book will help you to write a better story.

Roselle Angwin
Dartmoor, June 1998

1 The Creative Writing Process

Living the writer's life

It seems to me that there are two sorts of writers.

The first kind writes purely for their own pleasure, scribbling as and when they feel so inclined. For these 'fair-weather writers' – and I mean no disparagement – the creations of their pens, or keyboards, are their own reward. Writing is a hobby rather than a major motivation, and as such is approached largely with anticipation and delight.

They're the lucky ones.

The second type writes because there is no choice. Writing is an obsession, an addiction, a love-affair, a *raison d'être* which may drive him or her mercilessly, frequently with a fair dose of angst amidst the delight.

Sooner or later this writer will come up against the burning desire to cohabit with this obsession. Spare-time dalliance is no longer enough. The creative form this impulse takes is the 'magnum opus' – usually a novel.

If you have picked up this book, you probably lean, consciously or otherwise, towards the latter category. Perhaps aversion therapy would be more appropriate than a handbook. Writing a novel, if you're serious about it, is a huge commitment, and following the course outlined in this book will involve you in some fairly intense and intensive work. Books like this one should carry a health warning.

Writing any book, but especially a work of the imagination such as a novel, requires that you become single-minded in your focus; that you immerse yourself totally in the world of the imagination and the lives of the characters that you have created. In order to bring the plot and people alive, you have to be prepared to invite this story into your home, share the kitchen, bedroom and bathroom with your characters, climb inside their minds, feel their feelings, act out their fantasies, suffer their tribulations. For the time that you are writing this book, these lives will be as real to you as your own.

In order to avoid being arrested, sectioned or petitioned for divorce, you need to find a way to do all this inside your own head whilst still remembering to eat, relate to your nearest and dearest, get the kids off to school and do the shopping – and probably hold down a job, too. It's like having lodgers, but worse because you are – or should be – emotionally involved with your characters. What's more, you're responsible for their deeds and feelings (if you've had children, you'll understand what I'm talking about). Brace yourself, too, for the sense of bereavement that washes over you when you've finished the writing, when your characters grow up and leave home. The loss is not just limited to that of your characters, either; for after all, where else can you create the perfect life for yourself? It's a shock to come back to what the French call *quotidiennité* – the everyday world and its mundane demands and imperfections.

To the outsider, writing may seem a glamorous occupation. The public face of literature revolves around awards such as the Booker Prize with its prestige and financial rewards, or the book launches with wine and famous names; non-writers imagine a life of divine inspiration punctuated by regular lunches with publishers, agents, film directors and the press.

The reality, of course, is quite different. Writers sweat blood to incubate, deliver and rear their words. Whilst the muse may, if you're lucky, descend with Promethean fire on gilded wings from time to time, most of the writing is sheer hard slog at unsociable hours. Whoever said that writing is 1 per cent inspiration and 99 per cent perspiration was being a little cynical – but only a little. As for wining and dining, many writers work without agents, some never get to meet their publishers, and only a small percentage of books published are given an official launch. And unless you manage to write a bestseller, writing won't make you rich.

Writing is a lonely business. It requires an iron will and strong friendships to resist the temptations of diversions such as evenings out and holidays. It requires sitting down at your desk, whether or not you feel like it. For many writers, the only time available is in the early hours of the morning or late at night. I wrote my first book to its six-month deadline (deadlines are wonderful things) by sitting down at my word processor at ten at night, after my daughter was in bed, having worked all day in the business I was then running. It's crucial that you enjoy solitude – or at least that you are comfortable with it – and that you defend your writing time not only against anyone else who doesn't understand and respect it, but also against your own diversions and displacement activities, inertia, failures of confidence and concerns about selfishness.

The Introduction raised some of the questions surrounding the reasons for reading. So why do we write? The inner compulsion spoken of above takes many forms. For some, the act of writing is cathartic. For others, it's enough to create something, to give it life. Some write to find out what they think, to inform themselves as much as to impart wisdom or information to others. Many write to make sense of their inner world or to find meaning in the outer world, or to find ways of allowing the two to approach each other. Some write because they have a burning need to communicate their vision; others simply to tell a story. It can also be a way of becoming more fully human, developing facets of oneself that have been hidden, giving shape and voice to aspects of the unconscious. We have a whole cast of sub-personalities down there in our depths; while there may not be room for them in our everyday life, we can give them space in our writing, and in doing so discover the treasure-house which lies in our unconscious. But ultimately, most people who write do so because they have to, because not to do so would be in some way a death.

Creativity

Anyone who creates performs a vital function in society. Without wishing to be too precious about it, in a way all artists, including writers, act as messengers, intermediaries between what is and what could be, between everyday life and the life of our dream world, our inner promptings. 'Artists,' says Ben Okri, 'are both shapers and diviners.' Creative inspiration has its genesis in the realms of the gods. In a world dominated by technology, consumerism and a reductionist, materialist viewpoint, creativity and the fire that it keeps alive, in an individual or in a society, has an increasingly crucial value. Adrienne Rich, speaking of the 'fierce charge, or desire' which generates, for instance, a poem, says that this in itself can be a means of saving your life. Whether you're writing fiction, poetry or a journal, the creative flame needs to be honoured, protected and nurtured, and it's a writer's business, right and indeed responsibility to do so. To create is to give life: to inspire, to offer hope, to validate feelings, to give permission, to hold up a mirror, to articulate a vision, to share dreams. Never underestimate the power of language.

There are undoubtedly connections between creativity and wellbeing. Those people who live the most fulfilled lives, actualizing their potential, tend to be the ones who are also the most creative in their approach. It's true that creative types often have more dramatic and extreme lives and experiences than other people. This may, however, not be an expression of neurosis; rather an indication of the values by which they live. Because they are not primarily motivated by the need to feel secure, they are perhaps prepared to take more risks, to extend themselves further. By choosing to sail closer to the wind than 'normal' people they open up more of themselves in the process to a wider, deeper experience of the world and themselves.

Words – powerful, dangerous things

Creating something generally involves the manipulation of matter from one form into another. The dynamic relationship between maker and object, if successful, allows a degree of creative partici-pation, however vicarious, on the part of an audience.

The writer, like the musician or composer and to a lesser extent the painter, makes something out of nothing. Words appear out of nowhere and disappear again, leaving a subtly changed universe. (They can, of course, be fixed in a symbolic form on paper, or recorded, to continue to affect all who hear or read them.) This is part of the enchantment of both words and music. Both touch us and move on, leaving us – if they've been successful – changed. But words, language, are primary. 'In the beginning was the word.' The shaping of sounds for the purposes of communication and convey-ing meaning into the unimaginably immense and sophisticated vocabulary which is the human language is an act of magic that sets us apart from other species.

Words make spells. They have the power to caress, bless, entrance, seduce, excite, hypnotize, terrify, arouse, uplift, punish, condemn. The right word at the right time can transform a situa-tion or an individual in a way that a hundred actions might not.

Words exert control; naming something fixes it, binds it. Their power is recognized: freedom of speech, a basic human right, is rarer than one might think. Historically, and indeed today, certain ways of using words have been outlawed in some places. The Nazis burned books. Salman Rushdie had a *fatwa* put upon him for his perceived attack on Islam in *The Satanic Verses*. Julia Casterton in *Creative Writing* says: 'Books can be dangerous because the reading and writing of them involves us in an exercise of intellectual freedom.' People who think for themselves and encourage others to do so can be a subversive influence.

So words, though they can be used playfully, should never be taken lightly.

The alchemy of words

Writing, says American writer and inspirational tutor Natalie Goldberg, is an act of discovery. She suggests that writers need to cultivate the art of approaching things as if for the first time, each time.

Writing a book is a journey, an adventure. Through writing and through reading we discover and rediscover the world and our relationship to it and with it. A book that is well written, original and imaginative can open doors for its readers to look out on a whole new universe, or to see their familiar universe redefined and become new and inviting. Words in a way reinvent the world. Goldberg says that a writer's job is 'to make the ordinary come alive'; to make the ordinary into the extraordinary. Original writing, in the words of David Lodge, 'by deviating from the conventional habitual ways of representing reality', allows us to perceive the world from a fresh angle, as if for the first time.

You know when you have read good creative writing. This is writing that leaps off the page at you, that hits you in the gut and behind the eyes and in the heart at the same time as imprinting itself in the intellect. This writing ignites something which in turn sets up a reaction in the emotions and in the body. There's a tingle along the spine, the hairs at your neck prickle. This kind of writing is paradoxical: on the one hand, its potency lies in its newness, its freshness, its ability to make us as readers or audience rethink, re-envision our world; simultaneously, it stirs in us the 'Aha!' response which we have when we come across a truth that we have always sensed existed and yet have never seen or heard or articulated. This kind of writing peels back a layer of the world to enable us to look

– really look – at what lies beneath; it offers us glimpses into secret realms, which flesh out the dimensions of our known world as we watch. This is, of course, part of what makes the classics classic.

What does this kind of creativity in writing require?

It needs a cultivated attention to and awareness of the world; the ability to see into the heart of things. It needs a willingness to let go of preconceptions and perceive things as they actually are, moment to moment, with the kind of wonder and curiosity that a child brings to experiences.

It needs a willingness to stalk the wild animals of imagination and inspiration; to learn their territory, watering-holes and habits, to gain their trust.

It requires an originality of theme, or at least an originality of approach to the subject matter.

It takes imaginative and exact use of language, with simultaneously a lateralness and freedom in the choice of vocabulary.

It needs powerful imagery, rooted in the concrete and the natural world.

It requires that for a little time at least the conscious mind stands on one side to allow the unconscious to offer up its fertile territory for investigation. 'The mind should be a cunning net that can catch the fishes of possibility,' says Okri. In the West, we are so concerned with doing that we forget how it is simply to be. With writing, you don't need to actually create the fish; you just need to be in the right place at the right time with your net to hand. The most you often need to do is merely to lift them out and cook them.

Writing is both an active and a passive process. The act of putting words on paper is the active part. The ideas will come of their own accord, once you know how to put yourself in the right place, get out of your own light and watch and wait. Often the most surprising and wonderful insights and imaginings happen when the conscious mind is either engaged in something else or freewheeling. You do not need to force this process, only to learn to make space for it. Part of the purpose of this book is to enable you to find ways to create the right climate for these conditions to flourish. There are exercises in each chapter which, hopefully, will further the creative process in your writing.

It's a bit like harvesting vegetables. All that growing goes on out of sight and largely below ground with minimal help or interference from you, other than the preparation and composting of the soil and the odd bit of judicious watering and weeding. It's quite a miraculous process, the alchemical working of the unconscious mind.

And, most of all, this kind of creativity in writing requires that the writer allows him- or herself to feel the full range of human emotions. Unless he or she is able to do this, the resultant writing will remain pale and unconvincing. To engage your reader you need to be able to imagine and articulate the whole spectrum of human experience.

Taking risks

'Living is a form of not being sure, not knowing what next or how. The moment you know how, you begin to die a little. The artist never entirely knows. We guess. We may be wrong, but we take leap after leap in the dark.' (Agnes de Mille)

If you want to write you need to be able to take risks – in your life and in your writing. If you only want to stay where you are, safe and secure, then you will only ever be a mediocre writer. You have to be prepared to stretch yourself; to look into the dark places, to be moved to tears and laughter, to be honest and truthful, to write about your anger, your pain, your memories, your fear, as well as your loves, your joys, your triumphs. Not that these things will necessarily go into your novels; merely that you'll be writing from a superficial place if you're not prepared to fully experience life and write from the depths of that experience. How can you write about falling in love, or the death of a child, or betrayal, or a car accident, or transformation, without at least being prepared to imagine how it would feel to experience these things?

And don't be afraid to get it wrong. Jazz saxophonist Coleman Hawkins reputedly said: 'If you don't make mistakes, you aren't really trying'.

There are times in one's writing, as in one's life, when the only thing you can do is jump, often with no idea of where you will land. There are no guarantees; and trying to find lasting security will only result in a deadening as you close yourself down tighter and tighter. With practice, you can learn to trust your impulses, your intuition, your imagination; the unconscious can generally be relied upon to come up with what it is you need. So trust yourself to take creative risks.

In the words of Brenda Ueland: 'Be bold, be free, be truthful.'

Imagination and the unconscious

I suggested in the Introduction that the creative self may be found in the borderlands between the unconscious realm of the intuitive imagination and the conscious realm of learned technique. A friend and colleague, the editor Richard Beaumont, says that for him writing is a fine balance between possession and objectivity. This, I think, sums it up. So words of imagination spring from an encounter between the emotional, image-based, lateral, instinctual right brain and the shaping ordering function of the logical, literal left brain. I also said that in the West we tend to overemphasize the latter and undervalue the former, thus cutting ourselves off to a large extent from the wisdom of the unconscious.

I'd like to look briefly here at ways of reconnecting with the unconscious.

Ted Hughes, in his foreword to a book by John Fairfax and John Moat (*The Way To Write*) and talking about the Arvon writing courses, says that when a writing student is put in possession of 'the creative self', two things in particular become much more interesting: the working of language and the use of literature. The discovery or rediscovery of the creative self 'brings about . . . in an organic and natural way, what years of orthodox English teaching almost inevitably fail to bring about except in the most artificial and external way'. Hughes goes on to say that a student is awakened to a new awareness of the real life of language, with all its dynamic power. Literature, he says, is then seen for what it is – a living organism conveying 'the psychological record of this drama of being alive', articulating and illuminating all the depth and breadth and subtlety of being human.

How we can meet the requirements of this creative self and find effective channels for its expression is the fundamental theme of this book.

Learning to pay attention to the creative promptings of the unconscious is an important first step. Robert Johnson, in *Inner Work*, suggests that there are two natural pathways for bridging the gap between the worlds of the unconscious and conscious mind. One is by *dreams*, the other is through the *imagination*.

Dreams

If you are not already in the habit of paying attention to your dreams, I strongly recommend that you start. Apart from their psychological usefulness in highlighting areas of your life which are calling for attention, they have a rôle to play in expanding the field of possibilities for nourishing your creative self. Get into the habit of recording them as soon as you wake in the morning. This serves a triple purpose: acknowledging the presence of the unconscious; opening a dialogue; and accustoming you to the natural language of the unconscious – symbols, feelings, moods. You may find as a bonus that scenes, situations and images from your dream world provide the raw material for later imaginative work. Whether this happens or not, recording your dreams in writing helps to keep the doors open.

Imagination

There is part of us that is hungry for flights of the imagination, to be free of the constraints of ego, logic and everyday concerns, to enter new realms and be shown new possibilities, other ways of living. Imagination, says Lindsay Clarke, is the connection between the individual and *anima mundi*, the soul of the world. Imagination *animates*.

Johnson says: 'Humans depend on the imagination's image-making power and its image-symbols for poetic imagery, literature, painting, sculpture, and essentially all artistic, philosophical and religious functioning.' He goes on to say that it's inconceivable that we could develop 'abstract intelligence, science, mathematics, logical reasoning, or even language' had we not the capacity to generate these image-symbols.

The imagination as an organ of communication, says Johnson, employs a highly refined, complex language of symbols to convey the promptings of the unconscious via images that are received by the conscious mind.

Learn to pay attention to this language. Take notice of your daydreams, fantasies, feelings and moods as well as spontaneous images and those little voices which whisper extraordinary ideas into your mind at the seemingly most inappropriate moments.

How else can we feed or free our imaginations?

- by steeping ourselves in art, music, theatre and film
- by listing all the places, situations or events which inspire us and then committing ourselves to making regular time for them
- by learning new creative skills such as playing an instrument, painting, pottery or sculpture
- by spending time with stimulating people
- by learning to think laterally (see workshop suggestions at the end of this chapter)

Ideas both feed and free this process. It goes without saying, I hope, that writers need also to be readers. Good literature and inspiring ideas speak to our imaginations. An idea is a living thing.

The unconscious – and its imaginative processes – enjoys playing. Have fun while you're doing all this. To start you off, here are a couple of word-games to encourage you to think laterally and give your imagination a treat. You can do them alone, but it's more stimulating, and enjoyable, to play them with others.

Writing practice

The first game was inspired by the hilariously wonderful *Meaning of Liff* by Douglas Adams and John Lloyd.

Take a place-name – any name, from anywhere. What might it mean? For instance (from the book):

COTTERSTOCK (n.): A piece of wood used to stir paint and thereafter stored uselessly in a shed in perpetuity.

HEANTON PUNCHARDON (n.): A violent argument which breaks out in the car on the way home from a party between a couple who have had to be polite to each other in company all evening.

LULWORTH (n.): Measure of conversation. A lulworth defines the amount of the length, loudness and embarrassment of a statement you make when everyone else in the room unaccountably stops talking at once.

The second game is Dictionary (this is also available in commercial card-game form as Chicanery). This one's best played with others, and you might wish to devise a scoring system.

Take a number of obscure words from a dictionary, along with their definitions (you'll need either enough dictionaries to go around, or enough time and patience to await your turn). Each person or team works with a different word. Don't share the original meaning of the word with anyone else except a team-mate if you're working in teams. Now make up a number of alternative definitions for these words – perhaps four. The idea is to read out these definitions along with the correct one for the other players to try and guess which is the original dictionary definition.

One way of scoring is for the author(s) to score a point for each definition of their own picked as the correct one, whilst the opposing (guessing) team gains a point if they guess correctly.

Here are some examples:

UMIAK

1   Name given to large Himalayan hairy horned beast by first Englishman to encounter it
2   An archaic word meaning butter churn
3   Indian name for falconer's hunting jesses
4   An open boat paddled by Eskimo women
5   An Eastern European prototype car
6   Floating jetsam found under iceberg
7   Turkish souk storeholder's hidden money-bag

(Number 4 is the dictionary definition.)

ULOTRICHOUS

1   Heavenly merit achieved on chanting after the Russian Orthodox equivalent of confession
2   Having one nostril more prominent than the other
3   Being verbally abusive in a public place
4   Inclined to romantic entanglement, extra-marital or otherwise
5   Having tightly-curled hair

(Number 5 is correct.)

Some words to start you off: STOICHOMETRY, ODON-TOGLOSSUM, LIGROIN, DARIOLE, COLURE, CASUIST, ALIQUOT and TURBARY.

2 Writing it Down

Making space

Most writers cannot afford the luxury of an office or studio away from the house, but it's hard working from home; there are too many distractions. It's a funny thing, but friends and family quite inadvertently view your working from home in a way that they wouldn't if you were working in an office elsewhere all day. It doesn't help, either, if you have to keep clearing your writing off the kitchen table to make way for domestic needs.

A corner which you can call your own is crucial. So if you can, set up a desk somewhere which you use exclusively for writing, and on which you can leave your papers undisturbed. It's much easier to get down to work if it's there waiting for you than if you have to go through the rigmarole of clearing a table, amassing your papers, research material or notes and finding your place before you can think about starting. For many people, the bedroom is the only available space, but this is not ideal, as the subconscious message then is that the bedroom is for working, and your brain may start to switch on each time you enter the room, even when the message should be to relax and sleep.

As important as the physical space is your attitude to your writing and the area in which you do it. If you can, put your desk near a window; whether you are able to or not, ensure that the light is good. It also helps if you make your workspace inviting, with fresh flowers, an inspiring picture or quotes from other writers. Your subconscious needs to know that you take this work seriously and are going to give it your best efforts.

In terms of commitment, what you are writing is, initially at least, of less importance than the act of writing itself. ('One story or poem doesn't matter one way or the other. It's the process of writing and life that matters . . . if the process is good, the end will be good,' says Natalie Goldberg.) Whatever your literary focus, make a pact with yourself that you will write for, say, a minimum of half an hour each weekday, or whatever works for you. If you need to get up half an hour earlier in order to do this, so be it. I warned you that the writer's life wasn't all honey and roses. It's a myth that writers write only as and when the muse takes them. If this were so, there would be far fewer books in the world, and virtually no newspapers or magazines. Having said that, because the emphasis in this book is on the creative imagination, one has to ask whether the world might be a better place if there were fewer publications of the pedestrian, unoriginal and frankly dull and uninspired variety. How to avoid falling into that trap is part of the purpose of this book.

For myself, I write poetry as and when the muse appears. I write fiction and non-fiction, however, just about every day, regardless of inspiration or otherwise, though undoubtedly my work is better when there is a modicum of inspiration behind it.

Before we move on, it's perhaps important to reiterate that making space for writing in your life is not just about snatching a moment and cramming a desk into a spare corner. It's about allowing a sense of spaciousness into your interior life, too, so that the flame may be lit and will have enough oxygen to glow brightly and gain strength. This needs practice and a certain amount of mindfulness; a writer needs to learn how to shut out the outside world and its demands and false busyness and turn inwards, towards the imaginative life.

Getting started

All you need for writing in principle, of course, is a notebook and pen. You can write anywhere – on the train, on holiday, in the bath,

in your lunch break. Compulsive writers do. Certainly it's important to carry a notebook with you wherever you go; for ideas, snippets of conversations, quotes, inspiring poems, records of the way
winter sunlight falls across the fields or on puddles, the exact shade
of blue of someone's scarf, the texture of a satsuma as you peel it
and its taste on your tongue. This is the stuff of which books are
made, eventually.

A common question from beginning writers is: do I need a
typewriter or word processor? To which, I'm sorry to say, the
answer is yes; at least if you're writing for publication. You may
prefer to write first drafts in longhand; that's fine. Bear in mind,
however, that there's scarcely an editor or publisher who will even
bother to glance at a manuscript written in longhand; it smacks of
the amateur, and if you don't take yourself seriously, why should
they? Then there's the expense of finding someone to type up your
finished work – always assuming they can read your writing –
which may amount to almost the same cost as buying a basic word
processor. Word processors are user-friendly on the whole, and
soon become addictive. If you're the kind of writer who doesn't
know what they want to say until they've written it, they're invaluable, as you can move whole chunks of writing around at will
without having to cross out, drain the correction fluid or retype.

It really helps to have goals and to establish a writing routine;
but make your targets achievable so that you feel good about what
you're doing rather than guilty if you fail.

Notice which time of day is your most creative, intellectually
vigorous time, and if you can rearrange other aspects of your life
to accommodate your writing at this time, do so. Incidentally,
burning essential oil of rosemary in your workroom can help
sharpen your mental processes, and there are other oils, such as
sandalwood and frankincense and some of the flower oils, which
seem to ease one's passage into the world of the imagination.

There are days when the writing flows and you write a couple
of thousand words before breakfast without even noticing. Often,
though, your designated half hour (or whatever) will be gone in a

flash with little to show for it. This is how it is; life is all ebb and flow and it's pointless despairing. The very act of sitting down at your desk at around the same time each day is in itself the best start that a writer can make on any creative project. On the days when the flow seems to have ebbed, sit down, pick up your pen or switch on your word processor and just write. Act 'as if'. Don't worry about what you're writing, just get some words down. You can always scrub them or bin them; but in the process of just writing, many people find they stumble upon what they want to say. It's a bit like the seventh sister of the Pleiades: you can see her best by focusing on something else to one side of her. You can trick or surprise the subconscious – or perhaps vice versa. To mix a metaphor, the act of merely opening the channels by writing something – anything – can yield a seam of gold.

There will be days when you don't know how to continue with your novel; sit down as usual and write something else instead. Later in this chapter are some suggestions for writing topics to keep your creative muscles stretched even when the novel seems to have ground temporarily to a halt. Bear in mind, too, that time spent thinking about your work, making notes and doing research is still working time – but try not to use it to procrastinate.

Writer's block and other diversions

I'm not sure I believe in writer's block. It's a luxury a professional writer can't afford, and it's amazing how something akin to block disappears as a deadline rushes nearer! The easiest cure I find, as I've already says, is to switch on the word processor. Of course there are times when your writing feels clumsy, dull and uninspired, just as there are times when you'd much rather watch television or go to the pub than write. These two things are, I suspect, at the bottom of what people call writer's block.

It's amazing what you can find to use as a diversion. Six days out of seven you may not even notice the dust in the house, let alone do anything about it. But as soon as you're just a little anxious about something you're in the middle of writing, cleaning the house or washing the dishes seems to be of paramount importance. And then it's time for another cup of coffee, and there's a phone call you ought to make . . . and maybe you'll just walk up to the postbox with that letter that's been hanging around for several days . . .

At times like this the following strategies may help:

- First, check whether you're just avoiding the discipline of writing or whether you've become stale. It's necessary to the writing process to allow the well to fill up again, as Hemingway described it. Your ideas need the mental equivalent of frequent fresh air. If you know that you're feeling empty, drained, determinedly turn your face away from your book and do something *practical*. For some, going for a walk always recharges their imaginative batteries. Chopping wood or gardening may help, or baking bread, making a cake, playing with children, clearing out a cupboard, going to a film or a concert. (Yes, I know I said beware of distractions. Just be aware of why you're choosing to do this: because your unconscious needs it, or because you've got to a sticky bit.) The more you occupy your conscious mind, the more the unconscious will beaver away for you. Keep your notebook to hand; your best ideas will come dancing in at the most inopportune moments: in the supermarket or when driving, in a meeting, in the middle of the night.
- Try and pace yourself. Hemingway's method of working, apparently, was to make himself stop writing around midday, even though he knew (or perhaps especially because he knew) what needed to be written next. It's said that he then occupied his time by being out in the garden, tending his beehives. He wouldn't allow himself to continue writing then until early the next day.

When training a young horse, there's a basic principle which a sympathetic trainer follows: to stop on a high note, when the horse is eager and keen to continue. The temptation as a writer is to write until the flow dries up; it may be more helpful, psychologically, to stop before this, so that you already know what you're going to say before you sit down again to continue.

- Kickstart your imagination by reading poetry or listening to music or going around an art gallery. Many people find that writing to classical music stimulates their imagination. If you have a regular meditation practice, this can help your writing tremendously. Active visualizations – guided meditations – are extremely helpful to a writer, both for direct inspiration and to help the well fill up. There is more about these in chapter five. It may be worth using a tape (see 'Useful Addresses').

- As I've already said, sit at your desk and write anyway; anything that comes to mind.

- Forget your novel for a few days but commit yourself to writing something every day for fifteen minutes. Try a 'stream-of-consciousness' as soon as you wake up (of which more later). This has three effects: you feel better for continuing to write; this in itself can loosen up your imaginative/mental muscles; and quite often you can dig up a nugget of gold this way if you don't think too hard about it.

- If none of these work for you, backtrack. You may need to think about what you're trying to do with the book. Are you happy about the storyline, clear about the plot, beginning, major turning points and ending? Has the middle gone soggy and do you need to inject something else to maintain suspense? Do you have the right central character and is he-she clear in your mind? Have you started at the right point? Are you resisting rewriting something that needs it? Are you just plain bored with what you're writing? Make notes, reassess what you're doing. Remind yourself what the central theme of the book is.

- Be ruthless with yourself. Are you scared, lazy, and avoiding or resisting the discipline of sitting down, thinking and writing? Anxious that you can't do it? Believe in yourself. Everyone feels like this at times, especially with creative work. Courage!

Good writing habits

There are writers who, while writing a major work, deliberately avoid reading anything by anyone else. I understand the admirable reasons behind this: that they don't wish to be influenced by other writers and/or risk plagiarism. However, I don't believe that any creative work ever arises in a vacuum. We are to a large extent what our experiences have made us, and this will include the hundreds of thousands of books we may have read in our lifetime, as well as all the ideas and philosophies we have absorbed. It's impossible to avoid influence completely, and on the whole plagiarism is unconscious in any case. There are only so many original themes in the world; what matters in literature is how well you make your subject your own, and then how well you express it.

Almost without exception, good writers are also avid readers. How can you expect to be able to judge the quality of your own work, let alone know whether it's publishable or not, unless you are able to recognize other people's talent? You need to be able not only to see what's being published, but also to recognize what makes the greats, the established and the contemporary classics, what they are. And the only way to do this is to read and read and read. If you do not have the kind of voracious appetite for words that involves reading even the cornflakes packet at breakfast, cultivate it. Whilst it's important to learn discrimination, it's also important to explore as wide a range of genres and writing styles as possible. I'm not asking you necessarily to assess and analyse the books you read, but it may be helpful to keep in mind the question: does this book offer me insights, enable me to look at things with a fresh eye, challenge my views of reality, engage me, deepen my understanding? You may find that as you sink deeper into your own writing, you will have an increased tendency to read books bifocally: on one level for entertainment, information, pleasure, insight or whatever your personal reasons for reading are, and on another level for the author's handling of the intricacies of plotting, style, characterization, dialogue and so forth.

All of this will ensure that you have a clearer, truer ear for recognizing your own voice.

So good writing habit number one is to read.

Equally important is to keep writing. Yes, I know you're writing a novel. It's not enough. If you were dancing *Swan Lake* you wouldn't expect to just get up on stage each night and suddenly be foot-perfect. You would do your warm-up exercises and then practise, practise, practise, over and over, day after day. 'Don't stop doing writing practice just because you're writing a novel,' says Goldberg. Writing practice, she says, is 'our wild forest where we gather energy before going to prune our garden, write our fine books and novels'.

Writing practise is the literary equivalent of playing scales.

Each person will have his or her own method of approach. I strongly suggest, though, that you develop a habit of writing in a free, uncensored way for ten to fifteen minutes of each day. The work that you produce here is not intended for public consumption, but purely to 'open the channels' between the conscious and the unconscious. (Having said that, some of the most powerful, moving writing from students in workshops has been this 'warm-up' writing.) To some extent, this is intended to be 'automatic writing' in the sense that you are leaving on one side considerations to do with content, making sense, syntax, punctuation and grammar – everything to do with shaping and structuring. Tidy writing is not what this work is about. Rather it's about giving free rein to our spontaneous inner emotional and imaginative processes – about which more later.

There are various different ways of doing this. You can write to music. You could take a line (or a phrase or a word or image) from a poem and follow that thread. You can use a word or a topic from the list given later in this chapter or devise one of your own. Try writing with your unaccustomed hand. Or you can just write.

Stream-of-consciousness writing

James Joyce and Virginia Woolf are often quoted as typifying 'stream-of-consciousness' writing. To my mind, their work sits halfway between what I think of as true stream-of-consciousness and structured writing – inevitably, perhaps, as their books are intended both to be read and to convey some sort of narrative, albeit highly individual.

The term is a bit of a misnomer, as actually what I'm talking about is stream-of-*un*consciousness. It's rather like a painter assembling a palette of experimental colours. This kind of 'freeflow' writing is particularly effective if you can write the moment you wake up, before a cup of tea, before anything; certainly before the day cuts in with its demands. At this time you are closer to the unconscious and its world of dreams and images, memories and feelings, and your writing will reflect this. You can do it anywhere, though – on a bus, in a café – just filling pages. Eventually you'll become reasonably adept at switching off the 'left-brain' logical, critical function and this practice can become like a meditation. Think of your writing hand as being an unquestioning camera, recording unconditionally whatever registers on the surface of your mind.

Don't expect – don't look for – dazzling writing. There may be some, but that's not the point. To start with you'll probably find yourself just writing stilted froth, regurgitated dross, day-to-day occurrences, thoughts, events. It's very hard to let go of tidy-mind consciousness, too; many people find this kind of writing difficult initially. Eventually, though, you'll cut through the superficialities and move below the surface and start discovering what you really want to say. This practice can become very important, and you may find yourself writing with unexpected vigour, colour and insight; and almost certainly you will find that the calibre of your 'proper' writing will take a quantum leap.

This is different from the usual journal-writing in that it is not intended to be merely a record of events or thoughts or feelings. It's intended to be a net in which you can 'catch the fishes of possibility' – which may include all of those things. You're dropping a berry on a thread, in the words of W.B. Yeats, into the pool of the subconscious and lifting whatever is there, ready to emerge.

There are some guidelines. First, don't *think*. This is extraordinarily hard, as all our educative processes are about just this. Thinking is a linear progression; the type of writing we're exploring here is more akin to a mosaic or a collage of word-pictures, lateral and not necessarily obviously linked one to the other. So leave the need to make sense outside the door when you do this. Allow images, feelings and memories to arise spontaneously and immediately and without thought note them down – this is the natural language of the subconscious.

Secondly, allow yourself to be a passenger rather than a driver. Follow the thread, wherever it leads you, however bizarre or unexpected the ideas. Allow your mind to jump around, make crazy connections, run where it will. Allow word-association to guide you. This is free time, off-the-lead time.

Thirdly, try not to be afraid of the darker images which may at times arise. If you feel sad or angry, write about it.

Fourthly and most importantly, once you've started don't stop writing until the time is up, and don't read your work back until you've finished. Keep the pen moving over the paper, writing down anything that comes into your head. If you get stuck, just write, 'I am stuck I am stuck I am stuck' until your hand comes up with something else to write, or go back to your opening phrase and see where it leads you this time. Follow it, trust it.

Perhaps it's important to add: don't judge your writing. Put it away and don't read it again for some days or even weeks.

Possible topics for writing practice

Sun, ice, fire, flint, crossing the border, bone, loss, holiday, dying, I remember, my mother says, attic, threshold, when it was over, once, stone, water, bread, on the train, corridor, first kiss, leaving, cave, church, cellar, orchard, in the garden, the last time, party . . . the list can, of course, go on *ad infinitum*. Make your own list for the times when you run short of ideas; choose ones to which you have some kind of feeling response. For this kind of writing you might like to use scrap paper or a recycled spiral-bound notebook. If you use good paper you might feel too inhibited to allow yourself to write whatever comes, because you can be sure that some of it at least will be rubbish (probably). Keep these exercises; apart from their interest value as a record of your inner life, you might like to look back and see how far you've come in terms of letting yourself free-wheel, and in originality of language, after a few months. And there's also the odd phrase which you might want to lift and use in something else, or as a starting point.

Examples

These are all stream-of-consciousness pieces written to a time-limit: the first one five minutes, the others three minutes each. None of them has been edited or revised. The first two pieces used lines from other people's work as starting points.

The first one took 'silence inside this circle of sound' from a poem by Gillian Clarke.

Silence inside this circle of sound
outside, the petulant wind, flinging rain like gravel against the window, sending squalls shrieking and wheezing down the chim-ney – brief flowers of steam bursting like gunshot from amongst these cinders
silence inside this circle of sound
the candle wavers and flickers, strengthens again, burns brightly even though you are not here
in the meadow the horses will be huddled under trees already stripped, rags of leaves skimming like flights of birds over their rumps, dreadlock tails flicking wet backs, rosettes of shorter hairs splayed muddy
in the garden the tree is bare of fruit, one moulding apple perhaps succumbing to the relentless lips of slugs – or do they have teeth – gums – over the roar of the storm I imagine I hear the munching

slobber – strange, slugs having mouths

the garden is a mouth, and the night

the dog is buried under the apple tree. I was digging the pit the day
R.'s bombshell letter arrived with the jolly whistling postman. The
ground was icebound – even the laurels frozen – and Christmas
might as well have been a foreign language

his card with its false cheer, tacky glitter

that mouth nearly swallowed me up; I nearly fell, kept falling, falling
into dark

'Mummy please don't let them bury me alive'

lighting a candle

you are not here

silence inside this circle of sound where I sit, stripped naked of
summer like the apple tree, awaiting winter

You can see that this is not great literature (the best bit is the starting line!), but the images conjure other images and old memories.
I like the picture of the slobbering slugs, steadily focused on their
own appetites irrespective of anything else, and the hissing rain-
drops making 'brief flowers of steam bursting like gunshot from
amongst these cinders', and the idea of the night as a mouth. This
was my own piece; I've underlined the phrases I liked in my original copy in case I find a use for them some time.

Inspired by the same poem but using a different line as a starting point ('chalking the slate floor') is a piece by a student, Chris
Tooke:

Chalking the slate floor with stones dust from the woodworm
shaking like pepper onto the polished floor hinting no warning like
a clanging bell of the danger one little beetle can wreak I think it's
a beetle that lays its eggs which hatch into worms that thread themselves into the panel churning along the gullies indiscriminate
making paths like feet through grassland or layers of leaves in a
wood this wood built around you your own little fortress waiting
to crumble at the threat of a beetle

The next piece, again by Chris Tooke, comes from a phrase given out in a workshop: 'when it was over'.

When it was over the deadly silence whistled through my head lines on the wire fence whispered like a current bent on your last word sly crusty word hard line on winter pelts of fur hung on the line like whispers tails hanging wet matted dung clinging on hindquarters like slime on a stick run through a stream lights flickered on the back wall lighting up the fallen stone the crevices filled with black spider eggs until a million tiny forms crawled along the hedge light catching brushing the jet of movement that clung in silvered lines on crumbling stone eyes on furrows whistling in droves and cream silk shadows draped webs taut between the doors and window frames like gossamer curtains flicked open with a tiny draught of air you were the whisper that called me back line upon line of fresh blowing thread your voice on a back burner waiting to be heard and recalled on some winter morning a flash of memory unasked for but suddenly there acute

Chris has a natural feel for imagery. Here she juxtaposes gentle poetic images – cream silk shadows, gossamer curtains – with more savage somewhat menacing images like the deadly silence, hanging pelts of fur and the black spider eggs, hooking my feelings. Her metaphors hint at the now-light, now-dark nature of human relationships. She draws a reader in, too, with the repetition of words and ideas.

The next piece is also by Chris. Here she wrote from her own images rather than using a phrase as a starting point; immediately prior to the writing I had read the group a number of poems by T.S. Eliot.

Reflect my hand in your hand against a bed of feathers and circled around your head a halo light from the window caught on the goosedown yellow from the picture frame holding your grandparents circled in gilt edged history warm reflection from their strange still faces upright figures looking down on your twisted yet relaxed frame lying as though waiting for something to happen eyes half closed against the thin shard of sunlight we cannot block out a sheet of thin Indian cotton transparent to your charms ice melting on warm thighs fold lines cast around your heart as though protecting that little piece you will not show me though sometimes I can feel its glow

Finally a piece using a phrase of Ben Okri's to start: 'there is a red wind in my head'.

There's a red wind in my head he said today and nothing I can do to brush it out It's like the desert came and walked all over trailing bits of itself across our days There's a red wind in my head and in my hair like wild catprints rattlesnake tracks thorny desert claws camel spoor The red wind shouts. I want – I want a paintbrush slosh it all over blue slow it down a bit lick spit stick it back where it belongs inside some book, inside some map Shut it There's a red wind in my head and all I see is blood today he said

Writing practice

Stream-of-consciousness

Give yourself a few minutes to scan through a book of poems or a novel until you find a phrase that inspires you. Shut yourself away somewhere quiet and jot down the phrase. Time yourself – set an alarm, perhaps; maybe three to five minutes for a first time – and following the guidelines above start writing and keep writing until the time is up.

Focusing – your novel

If you've already started writing your novel you'll have some kind of working method set up, though you'll probably benefit from what I'm about to suggest.

Buy yourself a notebook for writing practice. In addition to this, buy a large ring-binder file and some file dividers. Mark the file with your working title (if you don't have one, make one up now; it doesn't have to be the final choice, but once more it will help you to take your writing seriously).

Make the first section the one where you keep all the exercises relating to working through this book but not directly connected with the novel. (These are different from writing practice work.)

Your second section will be details of plot, blurb, synopsis and so forth.

The third section will be your list of chapters. Take four or five sheets of A4 paper, and allowing a quarter or half a page per chapter, write the numbers in the margin: 1–12 or so. If you know what your beginning and ending are going to be, and roughly where the major scenes come, pencil them in accordingly (you can always swop them around later). This will start to give you a feel for the shape of the book; you'll probably find this immensely helpful. As you write each chapter, whether or not you write them sequentially, keep details on these sheets of the main events and characters in this chapter, their ages, physical appearance at the time of writing, location etc.

The fourth section is your character-portrait section, and the fifth will be for general notes, ideas and brief scenes which have yet to find their right place in the book. The final section will be for the actual novel.

Your first exercise (for the first section of your folder) is brief. Question yourself as follows, set yourself goals and note this all down.

1 List all the kinds of books you tend to read.
2 Describe in general terms the kind of book you'd most like to write, in fifty words.
3 What would you like to have achieved by the end of this book?

The obvious answer, of course, is to be well on the way to completing a novel. There are other possibilities, though:

- to take yourself seriously as a writer
- to have been writing daily
- to have developed your creative and imaginative powers
- to have dreamt up the plot for a second book

4 Why do you read novels?
5 Why do you want to write one? (Be honest!)
6 How much writing time are you going to try to commit to the novel each day/week?
7 How are you going to go about writing practice?

These may all seem to be trivial questions, but they serve to focus your intent and the act of writing down the answers is a message to your subconscious of this intent. Do it now, before you read on and before your good intentions get swept away.

3 Starting the Novel

Secret Lives

A significant function of the novel is the privileged access we gain, as E.M. Forster pointed out in *Aspects of the Novel*, into the secret interior of the characters portrayed. If the characters are well portrayed, we are able to lose ourselves, and the concerns of our own lives, in the life of someone else in a way that is rare in 'real' life. How hard it is to truly understand another, remarked Forster, to reveal ourselves even when we really want to, to enter into someone else's life. Intimacy, he says, is 'a makeshift'; perfect intimacy, it seems, an impossibility. In the novel, however, we can enter the life of another fully.

What's more, we can remake history. Fiction goes beyond the mere statement of fact, the cataloguing of events, and allows us to imagine the normally invisible human aspects: the emotions, reactions, thoughts and imaginings of the characters. Where the historian records, the novelist creates. The chronicle of events in a person's life, made up of observable actions and spoken thoughts, what we could call his or her history, is the aspect which we most commonly share, with glimpses now and then of what makes the person 'tick'. The other, more hidden side of a person's life, that which is made up of 'pure passions, dreams, joys, sorrows and self-communings', along with fantasies, imaginings, visions or spiritual aspirations, doubts and fears, which 'politeness or shame prevent him from mentioning' we can only imagine, unless the other person chooses to share them with us. A novel can and should portray both the 'surface' life of a character, and the inner life. The expression of this other side of human nature is perhaps a novel's strength and major attraction.

Forster makes much of the fact that the speciality of the novel is this glimpse into private lives: 'The novelist can talk about his characters as well as through them; or can arrange for us to listen when they talk to themselves . . . He can descend and peer into the subconscious [of the character]', laying it all bare for us to witness. The novelist, of course, manipulates the characters, the story, and also the audience, according to what he or she wishes to convey, to achieve.

Characters and plots

What do you wish to convey? What story are you wanting to tell? Why? It helps to be clear about all this from the start. If you can remain focused on your storyline and your intention in telling the story it will add to the coherence and the cohesiveness of your novel.

A decision you will need to make early on – if it's not already been decided by the nature of the book – is whether your interest is largely in development of plot or development of character.

While all, or certainly most, novels of course contain both characters and plot, there are nonetheless two distinct types: those which are action-driven, where the plot is the most important thing, and those which are character-driven. So the focus is different. In an action-driven book, the characters exist largely as tools to develop the action, and they tend, to a greater or lesser extent and perhaps necessarily, to fall into recognizable stereotypes. Because the thrust of the book is the resolution of the plot, the characters will not necessarily be changed by events. In a character-driven book, the plot acts as a vehicle for the characters to develop, change and grow, and it is not so important that the book is gripping and dramatic.

So we have two strands, one of which is normally subservient to the other. Ronald Tobias in *Twenty Master Plots and How to Build Them*, defines them thus:

- the pattern of plot, where the dynamic force of the storyline will guide you through the action
- the pattern of character, where the actors in the plot provide a dynamic force of behaviour that will guide you through your characters' intent and motivation.

Bearing in mind that in actuality these strands are not separated quite as clearly as I've just described, which interests you most, action or psychology? Until you have gained experience in both approaches, you may be best initially following your natural inclinations.

Each has its own dangers. If the book is all action, it's easy for the characters to become too flat, too stereotypical – puppets whose actions are superficial and not always credible in terms of real people. However, as long as the plot is sufficiently imaginative and suspenseful, readers can be persuaded to suspend their disbelief.

If the book is wrapped up in the psychology of the characters, the danger is that it becomes merely an exposition of navel-gazing intensity, or simply a series of minor incidents seemingly unconnected and rambling, with no strong storyline.

The writing of the novel, whatever its emphasis, of course, requires the same overall approach, as the guidelines apply to both; one instance is the need to generate tension. Whether your book is plot- or character-driven, the development of the story is likely, as an example, to require that your main character finds her-himself at least once, and probably more often, between a rock and a hard place. Both styles depend on the novelist's ability to set up a situation, generate tension, and offer some kind of resolution.

A good novelist, clearly, will pay attention to both plot and character development, whilst managing to keep the writing uncluttered. It is usually discernible, however, which is the important factor for any given novelist. Getting the balance right between weight of plot and weight of character means that inevitably one or other of them occasionally suffers. Becoming aware of when and how this happens will enable you to make adjustments.

'Genre' or 'contemporary' novel?

It's probably true to say that the 'genre' novels such as sci-fi, fantasy, horror, crime, historical, westerns and romance, are on the whole plot-driven. Contemporary and literary novels tend to lean the other way, although they will have elements of one or several genres in their structure.

Whilst there will probably always be a market for the plot-driven book, a glance at the shelves in any major bookstore will show the increased popularity of books where character-portrayal is paramount. There has been a shift in the reading public's tastes over the last ten or twenty years, away from genre novels and towards what is loosely described as the 'contemporary' novel, which has at its core the interactions and complexities of human relationship in all its shapes and forms, whether that relationship is to other people, to the wider world or to oneself – usually all three.

The major difference is in the emphasis, and perhaps also the purpose. A detective story, for instance, or the novels of say Dick Francis or Mary Stewart, may be intended primarily as 'a good read', gripping readers right up until the last page. We are less concerned with the characters themselves than with their position in relationship to the plot. They are vehicles. We expect to see the story resolved, and we are likely to remember the book because we remember the plot.

On the other hand a novel such as Lindsay Clarke's *Alice's Masque* explores the nature of male/female relationships as well as the mysteries and phenomena of the natural world, and is concerned with the growth and transformation of the central character. The questions raised about the nature of the world and our relation to it, and our empathy or otherwise with the characters – in other words the feeling tone and the philosophical undercurrents – may be what stay in our mind afterwards. In this case, the plot is a vehicle for the exploration of character and idea. The contemporary novel with literary overtones tends to concern itself with one or two strong characters attempting to make their place in the world. D.H. Lawrence was an exponent of this, as are Iris Murdoch, Helen Dunmore and A.S. Byatt, perhaps also Julian Barnes.

Having said all that, the categories are clearly less well defined than I have portrayed them here. How would you categorize the novels of Jane Austen and the Brontës, or Thomas Hardy? Many modern novelists have a foot in both camps. Joanna Trollope is one; maybe Jane Smiley and John Fowles. Where do you put *The English Patient* as a book, and as a film – and *The Horse Whisperer*? Popular novelist Dorothy Dunnett recreates the historical world through an adventure story and a plethora of colourful characters, and while her books do not pretend to be about the world of ideas and possibilities, her skilful handling of both plot and characterization, as well as her formidable historical knowledge, allows us to feel we are involved in the life of the characters.

There are also, novels which refuse to be categorized according to the usual conceptions; Jeanette Winterson's work is an example of this. These more experimental novels are largely outside the scope of this book.

What is of importance in exploring ways of writing a novel is that if you choose to break the rules, you should do it consciously and deliberately, which of course means knowing what the rules are in the first place. As in any artistic discipline – dance, painting, music, photography, poetry – the best exponents are often those who have the classical training to be able to choose what to keep and what to jettison. The purpose of this book is to equip you to make some of these choices as informed decisions. (The danger, of course, is the formulaic repetition of a set of rules: writing by numbers.)

Whose story?

It's important, too, to know from the outset through whose eyes you wish to follow the story. We'll look in some detail at both viewpoint and developing characters later on, but for now there are some basic guidelines to explore.

Who is the main protagonist in this story? In other words, with which character do you as novelist have the most sympathy? With whom can you most identify or in whom are you most interested? As a first-time novelist, it's a good idea not to clutter your work with too many actors, and it's crucial that you pick the right main character for your purposes, or you may find that your book stutters to an untimely halt. This is not only important for you as a writer, but also for your reader. Even an anti-hero must engage our interest and to some extent our sympathy – we must want to know how he or she makes out.

Which brings us on to a brief look at viewpoint. In chapter seven we'll discuss the pros and cons of prospective viewpoints. For now, we'll explore the main possibilities.

The first and probably the most common as well as the easiest is that you follow the story through one person's eyes, but as if you're reporting. This will be a limited third-person narrative, and following the conventions we have talked about, you as narrator will have the ability to see inside this character's head and be privy to his or her feelings. The story you are telling will be unfolding from this character's perspective only, so that although you will be reporting on the actions of other characters, you will not be able to divine their feelings or unspoken thoughts, except inasmuch as they are reflected through the main character's perspective and experiences. In other words, you will only have access to the interior life of your main character.

The second is that you follow the main character's life in a first-person narrative, as if you are the 'I' of the story. You will have even less access to others' thoughts and actions, as you are limited to narrating only those scenes in which your protagonist is directly involved.

You may choose to follow two or more characters' stories with equal attention throughout the book; this is less easy to do convincingly, but it can work well as long as you show your readers your intention fairly early on, and keep some kind of consistency in the structure of the telling of the story; for instance, alternating chapters. This has its own challenges and requires a certain amount of (extra) skill and juggling.

The fourth main possibility is an extension of the third, where you as narrator take a 'god's-eye' view and dip in and out of as many characters' lives in as much detail as you wish – the so-called omniscient viewpoint.

The choice is of course your own, and some stories lend themselves to one way, others to another. Just be clear about which fits your ideas most nearly.

Past or present?

A further decision you will have to take on commencing your novel is whether you will be writing in the past or present tense. As a beginning writer you may find yourself switching between tenses unconsciously – keep an eye open for this. You can, of course, choose to set the main part of your story in the present tense, using the past tense in the case of flashbacks. As long as you are clear and your reader is clear about when the events depicted are happening, this works fine, but you're laying yourself open to the possibility of confusion, and good advice to a first-time novelist is to stick with one tense.

Which one? Once again, each has its strengths and weaknesses, as well as its advocates and opponents. The past tense is the most common and perhaps the smoothest; if the writing is strong enough we are held by the story and can immerse ourselves in it as if it were unfolding before our eyes. Its weakness is that it can lend a certain detachment to the reader, whereas a present-tense narrative is more immediate, arguably more grabbing. We can immerse ourselves in it. Many writers write successfully in the present tense; however, it's my impression that many readers dislike this device intensely. When we read, we understand that it's a 'given' that the story we are being asked to believe in has already happened; I'm not sure how much using the present tense helpfully adds to this. The governing criterion is surely whether the tense intrudes or obtrudes in any way. If it does, change it; or at least try another route.

Approaches to writing

Somerset Maugham said: 'There are three rules for writing a novel. Unfortunately, no-one knows what they are'. When it comes to writing, you're on your own, and it's a question of muddling through in whatever way suits you best. Ultimately, the process is alchemical rather than formulaic – provided you have roughly the right ingredients in roughly the right order and proportions and you are prepared to put in a lot of blood, sweat and tears and sprinkle on a good handful of inspiration and imagination, you're well on the way. Somewhere along the line you find you have shaken the bottle without really noticing and the thing starts to take shape.

It seems that writers divide roughly into four camps. There are those who plot, plan, structure and write hundreds of pages of notes before they even start to shape a novel from them. Their approach is often clear and objective and the form is easy, as virtually all the work is done first.

There are those who just sit and write. They start with an inspired moment and just write from there, often without any idea of direction, shape, plot, outcome or even characters, trusting that these will appear as they write. If you are one of the latter type, you will know that almost miraculously the thing does take shape for you, without much apparent construction from you. This type worries about shape, structure and 'does it work?' only once the writing's been done. Unless, however, they're prepared to revise and redraft, they're often an editor's nightmare.

A third type writes key scenes, whether or not they are obviously connected. The hard slog, for them, involves linking the scenes in such a way as to make a story.

There's a fourth way, which is also my own. I have an idea of the main character or two, an intuition of the kinds of issues I want to explore, a rough outline in my head, or, better, on paper, and a sense of the ending. From there, I find a strong opening and beginning page, and let it write itself. It helps to be clear about plot and focus first, and early on — say around chapter three — I will make character-portraits of the two or three main people in my story. At around this time, too, I'll sketch out a synopsis from the chapter outlines detailed in chapter two.

You will know which approach will suit you best, and also which one it might be helpful to adopt.

Setting

The setting for your book, the backdrop against which the characters interact and the plot unfolds, is also an important consideration. Attention to setting will throw your story into relief, give it a three-dimensional shape, especially if you are able to conjure up sensory impressions for a reader. A book which does not build a setting has an unreal, shadowy quality to it which strains our credibility. Events never happen in a vacuum, but it's surprising how many new writers forget this.

E. Annie Proulx in her Pulitzer prizewinner *The Shipping News*, set in Newfoundland, sprinkles her narrative with frequent detailed but minimal descriptions of place, language used to capture scenes, smells, textures, mood:

> The short parade to Flour Sack Cove, take-out coffee slopping down dashboards, steering wheels gritty with doughnut sugar . . . The North tilted towards the sun. As the light unfolded, a milky patina of phytoplankton bloomed over the offshore banks along the collision line of the salt Gulf Stream and the brack Labrador Current . . . Rain-coloured distance . . . A deep smell to the air, some elusive taste that made him put in conscious breaths. Sky the straw-coloured ichor that seeps from a wound. Rust blossoms along the station wagon's door panels.

Throughout the book the harshness of the Newfoundland landscape and climate is contrasted with the fragility of human lives and loves:

> A few torn pieces of early morning cloud the shape and colour of salmon fillets. The tender greenish sky hardening as they drove between high snowbanks. A rim of light flooded up, drenched the car. Quoyle's yellow hands with bronze hairs, holding the wheel, Wavey's maroon serge suit like cloth of gold. Then it was ordinary daylight, the black and white landscape of ice, snow, rock and sky.

Whenever possible, choose settings that you know well and can picture. Readers are forgiving with certain parameters, as long as an author does not stretch beyond bounds their ability to believe in the book. However, setting a story in a location that the reader happens to know well when it is obvious that the writer does not, is virtually guaranteed to alienate or lose that reader. Make it your business to find out as much as you can about the place or places in which most of your action happens. There really is no substitute for a visit, preferably notebook and camera in hand. Drawing on childhood memories is not enough; if your book is set in the 1990s the playing-fields you remember may well have become a multi-storey car park, and the convent school metamorphosed into a block of flats.

It helps to have pictures of the setting, and maybe images related to it or photos of people who have some of the same physical characteristics as your characters in front of you as you write.

Bring yourself back frequently to imagined – or recorded – sense-impressions of the place. Try and construct pictures and images for your readers, bring the place alive (see the writing practice exercises at the end of this chapter). It's worth checking out how other writers tackle this. It doesn't take much to set a scene.

He'd left the open land behind him now. The city closed in. Waste lots. The desolate backs of tenements, row upon row, raw and unfinished, smoke-soiled, pipework bent and poking like fractured limbs. Rusty security fences impounding flattened scrap cars, naked in their uselessness. Gunmetal gas silos like strange preying giant insects from a nightmare future.

Noise pounded him on all sides; the rain drumming on the roof, battering the windscreen; the roar of the traffic and the nearby airport, and a deep electric thrumming which he imagined for a moment to be coming from the earth itself. He supposed it was the noise of the city, and the perpetual clashing of her inhabitants, life grinding on life. His heart was thumping with anticipation, with terror.

Take a look at these extracts from *As I Walked Out One Midsummer Morning* by that master of descriptive writing, Laurie Lee:

Then one day I noticed a long low cloud lifting slowly above the southern horizon, a purple haze above the quivering plain – the first sign of the approaching Sierras. After the monotonous wheatfields it was like a landfall, the distant coastline of another country . . . cool winds were blowing down from its peaks, and the plain was lifting into little hills, and by the next afternoon I'd left the wheat behind me and entered a world of Nordic pinewoods. Here I slipped off the heat like a sweat-soaked shirt and slept an hour among the resinous trees – a fresh green smell as sweet as menthol compared with the animal reek of the plain. I noticed that each tree, slashed with a pattern of fishbone cuts, was bleeding gum into little cups. The wounded trunks seemed to be running with drops of amber, stinging the air with the piercing scent, while some of the older trees, bled dry and abandoned, curled in spirals like burning paper. But it was a good place to sleep; the wood was empty of flies, who had learnt to avoid its sticky snares, and the afternoon sun sucked up the flavour of each tree till the whole wood swam in incense like a church.

Lee brings the same picture-conjuring talent to his descriptions of humans, too, even secondhand, as it were:

The deaf-mute boy Alonso, who I . . . met in the market and whose restless face and body built up images like a silent movie. He described his family in mime, patting their several heads, and suddenly one could see them in a row beside him – his handsome father, his coughing consumptive mother, fighting brothers and sly young sister. There was also a sickly baby, its head lolling back, and two dead ones, packed into little boxes – the boy set their limbs stiffly, sprinkled them with prayers, closed their eyes, and laid them away with a shrug.

In the market, too, I met Queipo, a beggar, whose hand had been bitten off by a mad dog in Madrid. Sometimes he'd lift up the red and wrinkled stump, bare his teeth, and bark at it savagely.

Lee is here writing thirty years after the event, yet his writing has the freshness, originality and vividness of imagery and language which allows us to picture the scene as if he'd taken us by the hand and led us to it in the here and now. He's not writing fiction – except inasmuch as memory adds its own stories – but a fiction writer needs to be equally able to paint these word-pictures.

How does Lee do it? One key is in his powerful use of observation; a reader feels as if Lee is at that moment standing in the wood, or communicating with Alonso. Surely Lee must take himself back to the time and place with all his senses as he writes. Then there is the use of imagery, metaphor and simile: 'I slipped off the heat like a sweat-soaked shirt'; the green smell of the pinewoods and the 'animal reek' of the plain; the 'fishbone cuts', and the sap like 'drops of amber'. He chooses his verbs with care; 'the afternoon sun *sucked* up the flavour', the trunks '*stinging* the air', Alonso '*sprinkling*' the dead babies with prayer. Despite his rich use of language, there is also an economy in it; in two sentences we have a clear and perfect picture of the most striking characteristics of Queipo the beggar.

Developing your eye and finding your voice

As a writer, all experience is grist to the mill. It's worth taking the time to capture scenes, thoughts, feelings, situations, conversations as soon as possible in words. You never know when you might be able to use them, and even if you don't, the practice is good for you. Train your eyes and ears to record. Explore how other writers do it, and experience what your own talents are. Perhaps you have an ear for humour or irony, perhaps you have a photographic memory, or a particular sensitivity to atmospheres – exploit these skills. Consciously try writing in a number of different styles and voices, switch perspectives from time to time and try looking out through another person's eyes at their world.

Often, we begin to write by imitating writers we admire. This is fine; it's only through writing that we begin to hear our own voice, find our own literary way. As you gain confidence in what you have to say, so you will also begin to trust the way in which you choose to say it.

I've talked a lot about decisions to be made before you start your novel. It's time, perhaps, to reiterate the need to differentiate between thinking about your writing and *doing* it. Of course a large part of the writing process involves the incubation of ideas, plotting, planning, thinking and rethinking. An even larger part means cajoling, threatening or rewarding yourself into getting the words down on paper, whether or not you know where you're going and regardless of whether you feel they're the right words. Just do it. It's no good waiting for the muse to appear like a genie out of a bottle; whilst she (or he) might grace you with an ephemeral presence, now and then, you can spend a lot of time attending on her, seducing her, pleading with her or even grabbing her by the throat and shutting her in with you. And there will be many, many times when she just doesn't respond, and you have to shut the door anyhow and get on with it.

Writing practice

Settings

Think of a place that you know and love well. Close your eyes and picture yourself in that place, absorbing all its details. Imagine that you want to describe it to someone dear to you, who is house-bound and blind. Write a description for them, based on what you see, hear, smell and can touch from your vantage point within that place.

Now do the same thing with a location you are using in your novel, whether it's real or imagined.

Plot versus character

Note down as many books as you can think of that you have read. Decide which of these is plot-driven, and which character-driven; how many are a balance of both?

Blurbs

Describe the essence of each of these books in between 150 and 200 words, as if you were writing the 'blurb' for the back jacket.

4   Inspiration, Observation, Imagination

Hunting and gathering

Ideas are everywhere, all the time. Everything, virtually, that we use, do or say has its inception in an idea. Some are great, some are not so wonderful. The point is, we live in a universe positively pulsating with ideas and possibilities.

The Oxford English Dictionary defines 'idea' thus.

- a conception or plan formed by mental effort
- a mental impression or notion; a concept
- a vague belief or fancy
- an intention, purpose or essential feature
- an archetype or pattern
- (philosophy) an externally existing pattern of which individual things in any class are imperfect copies
- a concept of pure reason which transcends experience

This is all right as far as it goes, which is not far enough. Let's stretch this a little further: I'm going to define 'idea' in terms of creative writing as including 'the originating spark' and 'a flash of inspiration'. In these definitions, idea has more in common with imagination than it does with reason, which is, I believe, how it should be.

Ideas, as I've already suggested, are a little like wild animals. Stalking them requires practice and patience, and a willingness to acquaint yourself over a period of time with their habits and behaviour, their signs and preferred times of day. Once you start to track animals, the forest comes alive for you in a way you would never have dreamed possible in the days when you weren't looking for them. It's a bit like driving a slightly obscure foreign car: until you possess one, you never see them; then suddenly the roads are congested with them. 'So much of seeing,' someone remarked, 'is looking for the expected, and tuning out the rest.' In order to open channels to the imagination, the natural realm of ideas, you need to unlearn old patterns and teach yourself different methods of perception. You need to train your eyes and your ears to be on the alert, and your normal mode of being may need to be left on one side.

Ideas are also seeds. Behind every creative work is the tiniest germ of an idea; the time and effort and patience and willingness to make compost and dig it in is what will allow this seed to develop its potential, once you've recognized it for what it is.

The problem for a writer is twofold: first, learning to perceive or receive ideas; secondly, finding a container or vehicle, a shape, for them once you've caught them.

I talked in chapter one about cultivating the ground of ideas through dreams, paying attention to feelings and moods, participating in activities which involve the senses and which feed the imagination; and in chapter two we looked at stream-of-consciousness writing. All these things help to open doors so that ideas may stream through to you. A bit like attending a jumble sale or going through a ragbag, there will be many you will discard; amongst them, though, you're more likely than not to find a piece of rare silk, some fancy buttons, maybe even a decent overcoat.

You should by now have a journal for writing practice. If you haven't already, you need now to buy a smallish, fattish notebook which you carry with you at all times. This is purely for jottings:

notes and ideas, scraps. In it will go words, phrases, lines, thoughts, imaginings, overheard or even misheard snippets, quotes, inspirations, observations, details, song lines, crazinesses. Think of this as your ragbag, or your 'rainy day notebook'.

Ideas, once recorded on paper, have a delightful knack of growing all by themselves. It's as if the act of putting them down on paper gives them permission to take shape. They take on a reality of their own. Many a novel has started in this way. Try and resist the temptation to keep reading back over your notes. Some germination has to start in the dark, and it never will if you keep digging the seeds up to check for roots. Allow some time to elapse, or use the notebook to dip into at random on the days when all inspiration for writing practice has fled you.

Sources for stories

A good guideline for the fiction writer is 'tell it like it isn't'. The art of telling it like it is belongs to non-fiction. Telling the truth is an exact science, like photojournalism; fiction is more like painting, ranging from the impressionistic to the purely abstract. The fiction writer transforms fact into something other: how it could be, how it might have been. If you do not innately have the knack of embroidery and exaggeration, you might want to try and acquire it. Embroidery, whatever you might feel about it morally in the 'real world', is what turns an anecdote into a story. Most novels are a blend of fact and fiction, one way or another.

Where do we go for our stories? Well, life: our own, our friends' and family's (but be careful), our neighbours', our community's, the wider world . . . stories are everywhere. Take a headline at random. Don't read the text; make up your own. (Thriller writer Richard Doyle wrote a whole book from one line in the *Daily Telegraph*.) Flip through a problem page in a magazine, or the personal columns of a paper. Let your imagination create a scenario from a vignette. Go to Shakespeare, the

Bible, mythology, fairy tales (Angela Carter and Margaret Atwood do this well), Ovid, Malory, Homer, anthropology, travel stories. Take a moment or an event in history. Rewrite the Gallic Wars or the story of Antony and Cleopatra as if you were a reporter from the *Sun* (though I'm not necessarily suggesting this would make good literature, only offering different ways of looking at events).

Remake it all. Define the theme, lift it, put it into a new story, a new venue, a new cast, a different time. Take an intriguing snippet of conversation, invent a context and a set of players. 'Borrow' from the subtexts in films or plays or musicals or even books. Tell the stories that *weren't* told (e.g. Stoppard's *Rosencrantz and Guildenstern Are Dead*). What about the rest of the lives of the two ugly sisters? How could you make the Pied Piper of Hamelin into a contemporary story?

In Kieslowski's three films based on the colours of the French flag, there's a tiny recurring motif which appears to have no relevance to the main text: a minute unidentified elderly woman attempting to reach on tiptoe to deposit her bottle in the bottle bank and failing, until finally, she manages it. (In the cinema where I saw the films, you could tell who had seen the previous ones from the small cheer that went up in the audience.) One day, I'll write her story.

Novelists are pretty shameless, really. Everything's a potential source: it's as if we drag a trawl through our lives with us. And why not? They say there's nothing new under the sun; it's a question of recreating it in the most original way possible. You can write about anything, as long as it intrigues you, arouses your curiosity or your wonder.

Other sources include your dreams and memories, your fantasies and your emotions. Write about a loss, an early memory, an embarrassment, a conflict. Write out a dream. Exaggerate. Try writing it in the immediacy of a dialogue – invent characters, invent a context, invent their history. Put it all in your ragbag rainy day notebook, let it incubate.

Powers of observation

So your ragbag contains a selection of scraps of the richest colours and textures. You need to put into this bag your observations as well as your recordings and imaginings. This means that when you pull out a scrap of fabric which may well be a thread from the gown of the visiting Queen of Sheba at the court of Solomon, you have the powers to describe the gown, the Queen and the court in a way that enables your audience to participate in your imaginings. In other words, you need to add substance to your imaginings; the substance of the material world. Exactly *what* shade of blue? What does it resemble? What does its texture remind you of? How does the gown hang?

If creative writing is a blend of imagination, observation, experience and 'factor X', you can at least develop your imagination and observational skills to the point at which the visitation of the unquantifiable 'factor X' is a frequent possibility (experience, of course, is a given).

Learn how to really look. You can help this process along by practising unaccustomed ways of looking. A useful exercise for painters is to spend time looking at the shapes made by the gaps *between* objects. Somehow it enables you to see the object itself more clearly, as if it brings it into focus. It's useful, too, for a writer for at least two reasons: one, it helps train your eye to look in a different way, looking for the unexpected, the unnoticed; two, it helps to set an object in context, it gives it a place in an overall scheme. It's easy, as a writer, to focus on foreground, on object or event, and forget that the imagined and described scene does not happen in a vacuum.

When you write from observation, try and describe exactly the scene or object or person or event in front of you, just as it is. Imagine you're perceiving it for the very first time and have no preconceptions or expectations to bring to it. Just note its characteristics. This is the equivalent of painting a detailed representational still life; it may have its limitations, but it's invaluable in terms of developing your eye and your hand to work in tandem.

You may want to bring a discipline to this kind of observation. Perhaps one day's observation exercises could focus on skin: the skin of a person, of an animal, of a fruit, of a tree, of a building. Another day you may want to note exactly how many different shades of green there are in the garden or the park, or write about a square foot of rock on the cliff path, or what happens to the muscles in your toes, your feet, your ankles, your calves, hips, knees each time you take a step. Or you could try tuning out the other senses and focusing just on sound. Write about the clatter of a metal dustbin lid, about traffic and aeroplanes and birds, about the thin wail of the next-door baby, about a thrush cracking a snail on a stone, about the sounds of cooking, typing, bathwater running, about the audience at a football match or swimmers in a pool. Listen to individual voices, listen to the whole massed choir of the world going on all around you. This is not, remember, about flights of fancy, the soaring heights of the imagination; purely a discipline in really seeing, hearing, recording things exactly as they are. Be precise.

Bringing the threads together

Imaginings, we could say, belong to our interior world. Observation is objective perception of the outer world: 'the act of noticing', 'the accurate watching and noting of phenomena as they occur'. The written word, in the case of the former, translates flights of fancy, feelings, fantasies, possibilities into a series of concrete marks on paper; in the case of the latter, it changes the solidly concrete form of external 'evidence' into a less objectively verifiable paper record. Creative writing, perhaps, consists of finding ways of linking the two.

The sometimes incoherent nature of our untrammelled imaginative ramblings, consisting, as it so often does in its rather dream-like way, of absurdities, sideways leaps and apparently unconnected imagery, can benefit from the structuring of factual reportage. Equally the latter, if it is not to end up as a dry rational piece of documentation which has little place in *creative* expression, needs the vitality and fire of the imagination.

A good practice is to switch between the two modes of perception – the one connected with intuition, the other connected with sensation – as an exercise (see 'Writing practice' below). You can write a piece firmly in one mode, then another piece from the other perspective. For our purposes here, it's worth differentiating and sticking strictly to each one in its own time. Say, for example, you're sitting on a park bench. In your first piece of writing, timed at five minutes, you record, as an impartial observer, all that you can perceive happening in the outside world around you. This includes 'static' happenings – noting the texture of the bench on which you're sitting, its feel against your clothes or your body, the colour or patterns of the leaves against the sky, the warmth of the sun on your hair as well as the blue-black gloss of the beetle crawling over your foot and the rhythmic thud of a jogger's trainers hitting tarmac.

In your second piece of writing, you are recording on paper the fleeting impressions, feelings and images thrown up from your inner world. You are still timing yourself, you are still sitting on your park bench, but the focus of your writing is totally inward. In our culture introspection is not generally given a high value or much time, so initially the act of looking inward may prove tricky. This can be cultivated, and activities such as yoga, tai chi and meditation all facilitate this, as does time alone.

These disciplines will have a different flavour, depending on whether you are in a building or outside. Try both.

The third way most nearly approaches the final objective of rounded fiction in which we are able to portray realistically the 'interior life' of our characters, and create a substantial world in which they move, eat, drink, love, hate and go about the business of living.

This can also form a useful exercise, where we allow our attention to be in two places at once – the outer world of stimuli and the inner one of response. Here we are recording in a more or less cohesive whole the events as registered camera-like by our powers of observation, and our feelings, images and imaginings in relation to them.

The simple observation of a dog, for instance, may conjure up different feeling responses in the observer. Noting these down in addition to the recording of the factual details – a large, hairy black-and-brown dog is barking and racing after a stick – will add a depth and an individuality to a written record. Perhaps the observer has recently lost a dog, and views the scene with a sad nostalgia; perhaps she has a deep distrust and fear of dogs, having been mauled by one as a toddler; perhaps he is a photographer who is captivated by the movement and vitality of the moment and views the scene aesthetically; perhaps she is a dog-hater whose response to 'dog' merely conjures up disgust and annoyance at the possibility of treading in dog-muck. Each person, then, will paint a different word-picture of this moment.

One of the bridges we make between the two worlds – observation and imagination, outer and inner – is likening something to something else. The object or event unfolding in front of us tugs, perhaps, the memory of a similar event or a similar feeling response in the 'I' who is observing and recording, and another time or place with its own set of events and responses suddenly emerges into the picture. This lateral approach adds another dimension.

In terms of the use of language, simile and metaphor can perform the function of linking the two worlds of observation and imagination. The observational method notes, say, that a dandelion is a bright yellow disc with a number of petals striking out all around it. The imagination may describe it as butter-yellow – butter being a metaphor used as an adjective – and liken it to the sun or a golden brooch or halo. Butter, sun, brooch, halo then all have their own connotations which they bring to the equation. Memory may offer other dimensions; perhaps as a child you kept a tortoise, and watched its slow, deliberate tongueing of dandelion flowers into its mouth. Maybe your father used to collect dandelions to make wine. Perhaps your association is in the present, with a feeling response – maybe they herald spring after a particularly difficult winter. Allow all these things to make themselves felt; allow your written world to be three-dimensional. If you can bring all these different aspects into your fiction-writing, you have a greater chance of creating for the reader a fuller picture of the moment than he or she would have if it had been merely a factual record, or only the promptings of someone's imagining with no anchor in the external world.

As always, of course, you can overdo it; try to strive for balance between simplicity and imagery.

Here are two extracts from a workshop, the first written inside a building, the second outside but with the attention confined to a very small area. Both allow an interplay between observation and imagination, but are rooted in the physical world.

I've come back inside after 'taking my mind for a walk'. So here; flowers a foot from my nose and a trio of glorious dancing swans, wooden and elegant, in front of the window.

This table has eyes; the flowers have eyes. Even the vase; golden eyes like a lion's. I feel warmed, feeling the world is looking at me as I am looking at it.

So many shapes. The rhomboids and rectangles of this simple vase, a surprising triangulated top, dashed yellow shapes. The squared lines of chairs and tables. The dipped ceiling with gold and green scrolled border, interlocking curves. The following smooth-ness of swan-shapes, the waves of wood-grain.

A waft of wood-smoke and sweet honeyed narcissus.

To be bursting out into this beautiful spring abundance.

And then I am lost in the eye of the tulip. A seven-petalled extravagance of blazing scarlet, daring and passionate, veined with darker crimson, pooled where petals overlap like layers of tissue-paper. A tide-line of palest pink and then an abrupt zigzagged inter-ruption of lemon-yellow and a startling streaked blue-green starry centre, like a frozen moment from a kaleidoscope. The petals are waxen, silky like thigh-skin; polished into a sheen where the light lies across them. Springing from the centre a black spiky crown, seven-legged like a spider just escaped with its life at the price of a leg. Out of this an arising, a triangular pistil, fleshy-pink and tipped. Crown and sceptre. A scattering of pollen.

I tear my eyes away; smell coffee, stand and stretch.

Outside again, and the eyes here, too – the watcher being watched. Choosing a couple of feet of wall an interesting confinement for me; a discipline in seeing. Not so much for my senses to roll in, drown in. Yet a million eyes in this surface; the eyes of holes, small holes where insects live, bigger ones at foot and roof. The eyes of lichen; ancient, slow, creeping feet claiming surfaces for their own, millimetre by millimetre. These eyes are rough but soft; silvery, olive, orange like dried egg-yolk, whitened like bleached bones.

Then the eyes of light and shade, protrusions pronounced, hollows and caverns thrown into darkness, lips into relief. Sandy to touch, barnacled; lines and small clefts and escarpments deflecting the fingers, running shivers up the skin. Close to the lichen is webbed and fronded like seaweed, puckered and creased, spread-eagled. I remember someone telling me that lichen is a cross between algae and fungus. Umbers, ochres, pinky-reds, slate-greys; shine of mica winking in the sun.

A million eyes, all watching me as I am watching them.

Writing with all the senses

An important component of most novels is what we might call the life of the senses. A fiction writer's success is intimately bound up with the skill he or she has for creating pictures in the mind of the reader. The physical world and the ability of the author to conjure up views, smells, sounds, textures and even tastes for a reader cannot be over-emphasized. This talent can and must be cultivated;

this is what will make a book three-dimensional, and give substance to its characters.

Good creative writing is firmly rooted in the world of the senses, and in the particular, says Julian Birkett in *Word Power*, rather than in generalized notions; in the concrete, not the abstract. A piece of writing which refers back to sense-impressions almost always has more impact than a piece of writing that is abstract. More of us, our being, both as reader and writer, is engaged in the former. 'What we respond to, with our senses as well as our minds, is a dramatic reconstruction of reality rather than an essay about it . . . the writing process is as much concerned with transformation of experience as with mere description.' The value, says Birkett, of a piece of writing is determined by whether it enables us to look at things with a fresh eye.

John Moat, the co-founder of the Arvon Foundation, said once that when he begins a piece of creative writing he makes a note of the five senses – seeing, hearing, tasting, touching, smelling – at the top right of the page he's working on. He'll refer back to this frequently, to anchor his writing. This is a good habit to adopt, certainly until it becomes second nature to use the senses as a component of language.

One way of practising this – second only to doing it with 'the real thing' – is to use a photograph or a postcard as a starting point for a narrative sketch, or a poem if that's your inclination. Take yourself into the scene depicted in your imagination, and recreate that scene in glorious 3D. What kinds of sounds would you hear? What are the main colours and shapes? Textures? What physical sensations might you feel? Any particular odours or scents? (Taste is not always as appropriate, but there are some scents – like salt wind – that you taste; or maybe the picture incorporates food or drink.) Write a few sentences for each sense, until you have built the world of the picture around you. You may want to stop there, or you may want to develop this into a piece of prose by asking yourself questions like: What's happening now? Why? What if? Who?

Grist to the mill

For a writer, everything's grist to the mill. Into the mill go observations and imaginings, and also of course our experiences. With the possible exception of potboilers written with a specific purpose – normally to make money – and therefore to a specific format, a novel will tend to reflect, even if only indirectly, a writer's own experiences and interests, and the picture of the world thus formed. Writing a novel is a way of making and remaking the world, for the author as much as the reader.

The seed-idea for many writers comes as a fragment of memory; an observed or experienced incident fleshed out in the imagination with the writer's key question: what if? What if an argument that you had with your brother *hadn't* been resolved in half an hour or two days, but had continued fermenting over months or years? What if you, or your brother, had a different temperament which spilt over into easy violence? What if the argument hadn't been about who won the squash game but about the arguably more serious implications of rivalry over a woman? What if the hidden agenda was that you were in love with your brother's wife?

Or let's say you have a strange experience in a foreign town, maybe an incident of *déjà vu*. Maybe you discover – or just imagine – later that there was a mystery of some kind surrounding the spot of your experience, maybe an unsolved murder. What if you accidentally and innocently stumble upon hidden evidence? Or what if you discover in yourself psychic powers which enable you to step back in time, or read others' minds? What if you become privy through these powers to suppressed information?

In this way, the incident, fairly minor in itself, can grow into a whole story. A prizewinning short story of my own, *Anniversary*, had at its core a theme from legend: the idea of a seal-woman. I set the story on an unspecified Scottish island and in the present day, and wrote it in such a way that it could be read simultaneously as an exploration of a marriage in the somewhat harsh climate of a northern island crofting lifestyle, and a story which hinted at supernatural explanations for the wife's appearance and disappearance. I like the idea of things not being as they seem. I drew on my own experiences and observations of a rural smallholding lifestyle, of the differing needs which partners may bring to a marriage and of an impression connected with scenery and atmosphere of a number of islands, some Scottish. I brought to this my love of rural landscapes and careful observation, and I clearly used my imagination to construct the story. The selkie or seal-woman idea presented itself about a page into the writing, at which point I rewrote the opening paragraph.

The originating spark, though, the seed-idea, came simply from two sentences plucked, as they say, out of thin air, which I set a writing group as an opening: 'It was high tide. At the water's edge, slightly salt-stained and still laced up, stood a pair of shoes.'

Pain and passion

Writing is an emotional, exposing business. If it has any substance to it, if it is to make an impact on a reader, you are likely to invest quite a lot of yourself in the writing. This risk-taking is a crucial part of the business. Whether or not you write directly about feelings, in a piece of creative writing you will need to be able to draw on your feeling experiences in order to create your characters and the events in their world.

Into the ragbag must go, with your imaginings and ideas, observations and sources, your feelings. It's quite cathartic on a personal level, too, to be able to write out your anger and your pain, your joy and your love, your doubts and fears. Easier said than done, I know, but it will help your writing along tremendously – not to mention your psychological health – if you allow yourself to really *feel* your feelings. Our culture doesn't easily encourage this. So when you get the chance, preferably as soon as you feel able after an 'emotional event', note down the incident and your feelings about it, as well as the physical sensations involved. Nobody else will see your notebook; and you never know when you might be able to draw on this and translate the incident into the life of one of your characters.

I am clearly not suggesting that a novel is an undigested mush of feelings. A perennial problem for the writer, too, is how to write about love and grief without falling into sentimentality. Often understatement works best – the gently direct matter-of-fact tone such as Michael Ondaatje uses in *The English Patient* when he's describing the burnt body of the main character and the responses of his self-appointed nurse can convey worlds of pain and compassion (see chapter eight).

Dan Franck, in *Separation*, employs this somehow slightly distant reporting tone throughout the whole book, which is what it says it is: a record of the last stages of a marriage. And yet we are drawn in to the agony of the couple, especially the man, from whose perspective the book is written. We *know* how he feels; by a clever combination of choice of incident – most of us can relate to the sense that someone is withdrawing from us, even if only through a distant adolescent memory – and the perceptiveness that comes either from having experienced it, or something like it, or from a profound understanding of human psychology, he enables us to step right into this man's head. And yet the writing is simple and unadorned; in fact he breaks many of the 'rules' that I've suggested. It's all foreground; he pays little attention to setting or context or sensory detail. Everything is subservient to the main thrust of the story, to which he brings an extraordinary feeling of intensity. It's a very un-English book (the author is in fact French).

Hanging out

So, in summary, much of what I have said about the creative writing process is about re-educating ourselves to really look, really listen, really hear, really feel. A writer's antennae need to be on constant alert, feeling out all possibilities, registering and logging them.

Keep your writer's ears and eyes with you at all times, along with the ubiquitous notebook. Cafés, bars, trains, buses, parks, parties all offer opportunities, potential stories. Get into the habit of noting down anything at all which catches your attention, however irrelevant it seems at the time. Like adding hot water to packet soup – but more exciting – a 'what if' sprinkled at a later stage onto a mere crumb of sentence may suddenly produce a snack, if not a meal.

This, of course, is a wonderful justification to do what the non-writing world thinks writers do all the time – spend a great deal of time over endless cups of coffee or glasses of beer listening in on other people's conversation, in the hopes of gleaning the perfect story.

Writing practice

Taking your mind for a walk

Choose a favourite walk. Stop at three key points for ten minutes each. At the first, concentrate on the wide picture only, and make an accurate record of all that you see and hear from this spot, including your general impressions of the landscape.

At the second point, concentrate on a very small area in close-up. Study this in detail, and note as much of it down as you can in ten minutes. Surprisingly, though the area is small, you will find that the more you look, the more you will see, and ten minutes may not feel enough.

At the third key point, allow yourself to become part of the picture rather than an observer, and record your feelings, impressions and responses to the landscape around you, allowing your imagination to suggest twists and turns and interpretations and perspectives.

You might like to take this walk in other weather, different times of day (or night) and other seasons, stopping at the same key points.

Objects – three exercises in perspective

Collect together two or three natural objects, such as shells, fruit, feathers, pebbles, fossils, pine cones, dried seed cases and the like. (You can, if you choose, include man-made objects like buttons or shoe-brushes or kitchen utensils.)

For each one, write three short pieces. All three require that you approach this object as if seeing it for the first time.

The first is an exact, almost scientific, objective description of the object, as if logging it for research cataloguing. Be as accurate as possible – if it's brown, exactly what shade of brown? Use as many senses as appropriate to give a full picture.

The second is the opposite. Imagine you are a visitor from another time or another planet who has never seen an object like this before. Allow your imagination free rein, let in curiosity and wonder. What might this object be? What can it do? How does it move? What could its function or purpose be?

The third is to assume the voice of this object (write in the first person) and address the world from its perspective. Rather like a riddle, the idea is to paint as full a picture as possible whilst still being somewhat lateral, obscure. If you prefer, choose a different object, such as a lobster pot, mug, ladder, coathook. Allow your imagination to go to town – be as pretentious as you like. Here is an example.

> I spend most of my life upside down. The one good thing is that the colour of my hair changes a lot – not that I've much say in it. If they forget to clean me I have the mother-and-father of a hangover the next day – so stiff there's no moving me.
>
> The not-so-good bits are all that wiggling to fill my hair up – breathing's not so easy – and then they beat hell out of me against

the wall for half a minute before dunking me back under. Don't ask my why – strange things, humans.

(This is a paintbrush, if you hadn't guessed.)

Four fifteen-minute exercises

• Write about a loss.
• Write about an early memory.
• Write out a dream.
• Write out the record of a conflict or disagreement you've recently had.

What if?

Take a strong emotion – fear, anger, jealousy, lust, betrayal, joy etc.

1 Write about it from personal experience. Try and relive it as you write; record remembered physical sensations as well as the intensity of the emotion.
2 Write about it as if it were an animal.
3 Use it as the core of a fictitious short story. Add a 'what if . . .'. Give the emotion to a different person in a different situation, but try and retain the intensity. Use the above notes if you like.

5 Right-brain Writing

Creativity and feeling

The momentous work done earlier this century by Dr Jung suggested that our 'normal' waking consciousness is only the tiny tip of an iceberg, or a small island in a vast ocean. The king of this island, the ruling force, is the ego; and surrounding this field of self-consciousness is the sea of the unconscious. Or, if you prefer, it is the enormous mass that forms the body of the iceberg.

For most of us, as I've mentioned, our main contact with the unconscious is through the realm of dreams. We meet it, too, through art and works of the imagination: paintings, music, theatre, story, dance.

Now and then it intrudes into our daily life – through daydreams for instance. Another example is when something stirs our feelings; we've all had the experience of finding ourselves delivering a sudden, passionate outburst on something that has without warning touched our feelings. We can all find ourselves, from time to time, caught up in strange moods, inexplicable depressions, feelings that seemed to descend on us from nowhere. Most of us, too, can recall a time when we've suddenly been affected by an atmosphere.

Once or twice, no doubt, you've been running through a scenario, a memory or a problem in your mind whilst driving; you arrive at your destination and realize that you have no idea how you got there. You've taken the necessary turns, stopped at the necessary lights and pedestrian crossings and found the correct roads; and yet when you get there you have no memory of the journey at all. No, I'm not talking about abduction by aliens – though there might be an explanation here somewhere for so-called abductions – but about 'automatic pilot'. Whilst your conscious mind was engaged in something absorbing, your unconscious mind stepped in and did the necessary work.

There are those times, too, when a scent, a word, a scene will provoke a long-lost memory or feeling, or an image.

The ego is somewhat threatened by the apparent chaos of this turbulent, untrammelled world. The ego likes to be in control, to have the reins tightly in hand, to steer and direct our lives towards survival. This part of ourselves doesn't really like to take too many risks; anything new and untried is perceived as possibly dangerous. It prefers things which can be easily categorized and which make sense and proceed in an orderly manner towards a predictable outcome. Its survival instinct is strong.

The function of normal consciousness – which is of course necessary – can also be labelled, for our purposes, 'left brain'. Left brain is logical, reasoning, linear and sequential, orderly. Left brain oversees our powers of discernment and discrimination. It deals in intellectual processes, progressions, critical functions and objectivity.

In our culture and our educational system, left brain is highly valued. Goal-orientated, it 'gets things done'. Its shortcoming – and its enemy – is the intuitive world of feelings, instincts and imagination.

Our creativity and our capacity to imagine, to feel, to love, are linked to another part of ourselves. The 'right brain' part of us, the world of the unconscious, actually provides the nourishment for all that we are, including the world of the ego, the conscious mind. They are not separate, although in the West we have forgotten to some extent how to move between them, how to build bridges.

One of the demands for a writer – and many writers manage this intuitively – is to move back and forth between these two worlds. We convert impressions into expressions. If we do it well, our work can offer a bridge for a reader to do the same. Deep down, we all have a yearning to lose ourselves – even momentarily – in this other world, this world of dreams and images, away from the 'red alert' state of the conscious mind. This is crucial, in fact, for health; a study a few years ago showed this. A number of student volunteers were monitored whilst sleeping. Although given enough sleep in terms of hours, they were woken up every time they entered a period of REM (rapid-eye-movement) sleep, the mode in which dreams occur. After a number of days of this, the subjects started hallucinating. The brain needs this vital recharging; if it doesn't get it in the normal way, it finds another route.

So where left brain is logical, right brain is irrational. Where left brain is reasonable and orderly (I have a theory that left-brain-ruled cultures developed queuing), right brain is emotional and chaotic. Where left brain is literal, right brain is lateral. Left brain needs to make sense and be grown-up; right brain needs wild flights of fancy and time to play. Right brain offers the images; left brain interprets and shapes them.

If left brain is critic, right brain is creator. The interaction between the two produces works of art. If the right prompts and inspires, the left channels and shapes. We need both; and we especially need to learn to access the right brain if we want our written work to be vital, exciting, surprising, original, and to have depth.

Chatterboxes and control freaks

The inspiring tutor Natalie Goldberg talks of 'monkeymind' and 'tidy mind'. These are good metaphors for two states of mind beyond which creative writers need to be able to travel.

Monkey mind is incessantly busy. It collects to itself and slavers over absolutely everything, soaking up information like a sponge, indiscriminately and voraciously. Much of what it devours – most, even – is trivial. Bombarded as we are with a constant stream of stimuli, our minds work overtime digesting the information and filtering out and processing what seems to be important. I'm reminded of the mussel, through whose shell about ten gallons of water pass a day in order for it to filter out the small quantity of minute particles on which it feeds. (An image offered by the right brain there.)

Monkey mind is the chatterbox. Monitor yourself for five minutes. There is constant 'white noise' which passes for thought – snippets of more important thoughts interspersed with a barrage of 'where did I put that?', 'is there time for this?', 'maybe a cup of tea', 'what shall I have for supper?', 'did she really mean that?', 'don't like his tie very much', 'must get in touch with . . .', 'damn, forgot to cancel the newspapers', 'that's a book I'd like to read', 'what was that noise?', 'looks like she's going to be late again'. You get the picture. We all do it. There is a connection here with what we discussed in chapter two, what has been called 'stream-of-consciousness' writing as exemplified by Virginia Woolf and James Joyce (though it is not exactly synonymous with what I mean by this). Here our view of the interior life of a character involves their interior monologue, too. Clearly, there is some selection going on in Woolf's and Joyce's writing in order to make the flow smooth and not too tedious.

Tidy mind is the control freak, the critic. This is the little voice – or sometimes a very loud one – that says: 'You can't write that. It doesn't make sense. Your mother-in-law might read it. You're writing rubbish. You'll never make a writer. What does that mean? Who do you think's going to want to read this? Go on, bin it.' Tidy mind – the critic – does have a part to play in writing, but in an editorial capacity *after* the creative work has been done. The critic/editor helps shape and structure the images and ideas in order to present them as clearly as possible with a view to conveying them to an audience.

Somehow you as writer need to find a way to bypass these two modes of thought, to find a path between them to what you actually want to say, to what is important.

The critic seems to respond well to being told to stay out of the way for a period of time. You can use psychological 'tricks' – Natalie Goldberg talks about visualizing sending the critic to the day-care centre while you get on with your creative writing! With groups I've found a useful image is to ask people to picture themselves leaving the critic outside the door of the writing room, which is then shut. The critic is only invited in when you want an editorial eye, and then dismissed again. Treat the internal critic as you would a well-meaning but overbearing and interfering busybody of a neighbour. 'I don't need your help right now, thank you.' You can always make a deal that you'll let the critic have a look-in later. Bribe him or her. This psycho-speak may all seem a bit over the top, but indulge it, play it up, make characters out of these internal functions. The right brain loves games like these.

The writer's use of meditation

I can't emphasize enough how helpful some kind of meditation process is in stilling the chatterbox. Though it's hard sometimes, especially at the beginning, learning to still and slow the mind pays dividends in many different areas.

One payoff is that, deprived of its habitual stimulus, monkey mind eventually goes to sleep for a while, though it has to be said not always without a grumble.

Meditation is not about suppressing anything. Meditation here is about finding ways of making a path through all the trivia to what lies underneath. It involves gaining a sense of proportion, and allowing other parts of the brain to come in. It enables the mind to change gear. It's not achieved by pushing out the unwanted thoughts; it's achieved by allowing them to pass by without grabbing at them, without attaching any importance to them in any way at all.

If this appeals to you, here are some suggestions.

Find yourself a quiet place and a time when a minimum of interruption will occur. You might want to unplug the phone and lock the front door.

Find a position that's comfortable. You have two options: to sit up or to lie down. They offer different things. If you lie down, the brain may get the message that you want to go to sleep. While this will be relaxing, it's not quite the same as meditating. On the other hand, when you're lying down the messages sent to the brain may allow you easier access to the unconscious, as is the case immediately before and after sleep. If you sit up, you are less likely to fall asleep and more likely to be in control. One way around this is to use the supine position for active imagination or visualizations (of which more later) and the sitting one for the purpose of stilling your mind.

If you sit, choose a comfortable chair which supports you upright. It's best if your surroundings, or at least your immediate view, aren't too interesting, unless you're going to close your eyes (which helps the process). Some people use something like a candle-flame as a focus – with their eyes open of course. Another way is just to bring your attention to your breath; just noticing the breath coming into the body and the breath leaving the body. Each time your mind wanders – and it does – just gently bring your attention back to the breath. Don't allow your critic in to berate you about this. If your mind wanders, you're not 'doing it wrong', you haven't failed – it's just the way the mind is. A meditation teacher I once had suggested picturing the mind as a wide blue sky, and the thoughts as clouds floating across it, which you notice but don't either hang on to or push away.

Each time it becomes a little easier; your attention span lengthens. As thoughts and feeling arise, notice them and let them pass by. You may find some useful images and ideas; you may not. The point is to still the surface chatter so that you can look beneath. The sense of relaxation and wellbeing is a bonus!

If you can, do this every day, starting with ten minutes and building up to as long as is comfortable. It's a good discipline to do immediately before writing, especially if you have got into the habit of stream-of-consciousness writing in the way that we explored in chapter two. You can use the meditation experience

84

itself and the thoughts and feelings which emerged during it for your warm-up practice.

Listening to the inner voices

One active benefit of meditation is that it allows the important things through. It makes space for the inner voices, which are otherwise lost, to have their say. It's helpful to get into the habit of paying attention to these voices, these promptings from the unconscious.

Meditation allows the space for you to learn to differentiate between the voices of habit and judgement and the intuitive wisdom which can inform your writing. Being quiet in this way is also a technique for solving knotty problems in your writing; if you have come unstuck (or become stuck) with a scene, a character, some plot development, stilling the mind can miraculously free up the processes. It opens a channel into the unconscious, which more often than not can offer you the solution, if you learn to listen to it. Often the answers we need are simply washed away in the flood of everyday trivia. It's not that you go into meditation worrying about the issue, the problem in what you're writing; you don't have to try to force the unconscious. You simply let other distractions melt away and make the space for the clearer inner voices to have their say. It can seem miraculous at times.

Active imagination

Before we explore this it's important to warn you: the unconscious, the imaginative realm, is powerful. It needs treating with respect and care. Sometimes it can be overwhelming, and if, as they say, you are of a nervous disposition, or are readily lost in fantasy, have recently been through a crisis or are feeling emotionally vulnerable or you have a history of nervous disorders, you may not wish to set up this kind of dialogue with the unconscious. Reading what I'm about to say, you might think I'm making a fuss about nothing; but don't underestimate the power of the unconscious. Some people prefer to do this kind of work with a professional: a therapist who works with personal development, maybe. An alternative is some kind of tape with guided meditations or visualizations on it; there are also books on the process (see 'Bibliography' and Useful Addresses').

Active imagination, like dreaming, is a way of accessing the unconscious. Unlike dreaming, though, it takes place when you are awake, and involves a dynamic exchange between the conscious mind and the unconscious. You are an active participant in the exchanges that take place. You have more control, therefore, than you do with a dream. If you are using a tape, for instance, you can simply switch it off if you have had enough. If you are finding it difficult or uncomfortable, stop. Go for a walk, read a book, have a snack. It's also different from passive or receptive imagination, such as daydreaming, where you merely sit back and allow the stream of fantasy to flow past you.

When emerging from a spell of active imagination, it's important to immerse yourself consciously back in the world of the flesh. Make some notes, have a cup of tea and a biscuit, stretch, take some exercise.

In your imagination you begin to talk to and interact with the images that appear. These images represent parts of yourself, often completely unknown parts. You have a whole cast of characters in there, living out their own dramas. What a treasure trove for a novelist! Cash in on it.

You can question or respond to the images or characters that appear. Get them talking to each other, and with you. Ask them who they are, what they want, what they have to say.

Psychology tells us that for each conscious function, we have a compensatory unconscious function. If we live our lives in an overly grown-up, serious and responsible way, inside us will be a character who is childlike, frivolous and playful. If we try to be a 'nice' person all the time, inside us will be a demon; or at least a stroppy, aggressive, demanding, selfish character. We can draw on these buried qualities to inform our writing. We can ask these qualities to become personified in our imagination, and draw on the character who appears. This character may tell us things we never consciously knew, express thoughts we didn't know we thought.

Here are a couple of suggestions for starting the process of active imagination (have your notebook handy). Whichever you use, take yourself to the quiet place we talked about in the section on meditation. If you want to use active visualization specifically to feed into your novel, it's a good idea to hold that intention in your mind before you start with any of these approaches, perhaps also mentally running through the characteristics or rôle in your book of the characters you want to meet. After the visualization, note down details of any characters who presented themselves to you, and now or at a later date, start to talk with them.

The first way is to use a guided visualization tape. You can buy one, or record one yourself from suggested exercises in the number of books which address these processes; or have a friend talk or read you through the process. If you have a friend you trust who might also be interested in this way of working, you could help each other with the process.

Another possibility is to think back over your recent dreams. Do any of the people in them remind you of any of your characters? If not, could you still draw on them for your writing? If so, 'call up' these characters in your imagination and start to talk with them; question them.

A third way is to go to a place – perhaps a setting or scene in your novel – in your imagination, and see what or who turns up.

A fourth way is to start 'cold', merely by emptying your mind and making a conscious space for images in connection with your fiction-writing, which you then explore. Make sure your unconscious knows your intent by repeating mentally the fact that you want to work with images appropriate to your novel (if that is your intent).

However you do it, don't forget to make notes. The easiest way is to jot down any physical characteristics, details or events that seem important, then to record any dialogue as it occurs. Identify who's speaking each time by a letter or symbol in the margin. You could, of course, also tape it if you speak it aloud – as long as you don't mind about sounding silly, or worse, crazy.

Remember that you are in control. Use your ego, if necessary, to set boundaries, to respond appropriately, to step in if necessary. You choose to enter this imaginative realm but you are not bound to stay stuck in it, or to leave your conscious mind and judgement out of the picture. Remember that you are not a powerless dreamer, but an active participant in this process. Do not allow your imagination to be hijacked by any of these imagined characters. Close the visualization when *you* are ready to. And take it seriously.

Writing to music

Music offers an easy entry into the right brain, the world of images and feelings, for most people. You will see from the following short workshop piece that this happens even when you think it can't or won't.

Right, Brian

Ethereal music again. Can't float today. I'm a lead weight. Or, a Turk's Head knot is filling my stomach. Something tugging, trying to unravel. I went well with the binbags this morning. Black, bursting, abandoned. Must get out of this. I turned a corner and there were the blackberries. Autumn and still July. The petunias are blown. He only took one suitcase. Tissues, tickets, take it. Incongruous, incongruity, incongruinfinity. Infinity music. Chant that never ends. Saxophone, sex music. Write around the wet patches. Inconsequential, incognito, in love, innuendo, incense, incensed.

(*Lyn Browne, 1997*)

The principle is simple – merely switch on some music and allow your hand to write whatever is there to be written, as with stream-of-consciousness writing. Don't force it, don't monitor it and don't stop writing till the music finishes. Obviously different kinds of music will stimulate different responses – switch between different kinds. I've never known this to fail to produce a written response; it's a good warm-up for any kind of writing.

You can of course use music as quiet background while you write your novel. For some this works well; others find it distracting. Words can be offputting, so try instrumental pieces first of all. One of the students on my first novel course wrote her book accompanied by the baroque viol music of Marais on her headphones; I use the Brandenburg concertos to facilitate my flow.

Art-inspired writing

Using paintings or photographs as a springboard is another way of accessing the unconscious. The easiest way is to use an art postcard.

The idea is to step into the picture. One way to start this off is to imagine yourself in the scene or landscape pictured with each of your senses in turn, as described in chapter four. What can you hear? What does it remind you of? What are the colours around you, the textures, the smells? Write a sentence or two from the perspective of each sense.

Then thinking as much as possible in images, similes and metaphors, create a scenario or story. What's happening here? Where is it? What's the date? The season? The time of day? The weather? This picture is a frozen moment; what's momentous about it? What's significant about the scene? Who are the inhabitants of this environment/landscape, pictured or invented? What is significant about this season, this time of day, this place, for them? What's happening right now this moment in this place? Who or what is just outside the boundaries of the picture? Any details you've missed? Anyone you want to introduce into this landscape?

How are you involved in it? Question; keep questioning until the well runs dry.

Refer back to your senses and your imagination as much as you can. Root the story in the concrete, not the abstract. You may find you've created a scene, a story or a landscape you can use in your fiction, but even if you haven't, it's good imaginative practice.

Memories, dreams, reflections

A useful thread to follow is that of an important memory, one that has an emotional charge attached to it. A related idea is to close your eyes and see yourself flipping through an imaginary book of memories, like a photograph album. Choose one or two to follow through and write about.

Here is another workshop piece (like the first one, unedited) following a memory.

Go back in time; write of a place well known, show every crack, every line, the colours, hues, tears, blood, sweat, grime. Triumphs, failures. Run your fingers along the grain of it, smell the scents, taste the bitter sweet harvest, dig for the nut, that hard, impenetrable place, held in chords [sic] bonded by time . . .

Head in hands, arms resting on knees, watching flames. Fire pictures fuse with thought. Hairs on the back of my neck rise. I smile; I sigh; alone in this state, where the tides meet, coiled in the ache of joy and grief. Smiles open the petals of the heart; sighs give black soul-birds flight.

my father's hands, strong, long, square fingers, veins sticking out like worms under the skin. Hairs, dark against brown skin, nails hard clipped. Secure, safe. They remain the yardstick by which I measure trust, in every man I meet.

my mother's fur coat. Soft, warm. The colour of honey in sunlight. Smelling of home, of her, and familiarity. Rippling when she moved, high above me, in that place where I now am, beyond fairies and pictures in the clouds. A sometimes sad place where people die . . ., as rainbows, all colour drained. Red, orange, yellow, green, blue, indigo, violet. The flames dance on. Her coat remains, hanging in my cupboard, for stroking when my heart is cold; though now there is sadness for the wee creatures . . . and no body to wear it.

the first book I ever read, *The Ascent of Everest*. Life IS; climbing mountains, exhilaration, expectation, effort, descent; then on towards another summit . . .

and there, half way up the hillside, I come, unexpectedly, upon a hanging lake, not seen from below, my feet trample the heather; stones placed in piles? No, they are the remains of cells, huts, inhabited long ago, when saints walked the earth and there was no need for fences. The light, silver on the water, insects hum and the air is heavy with the scent of past fires, and mists rising with the lark to greet dawns long gone. I am alone, and yet, not, in this place between earth and heaven, where fish dance in the lake and sheep graze, barely acknowledging my attention of their quiet cropping. A place of solitude, quiet contemplation, timeless, inhabited, yet deserted. Cloud-shadows race for distant mountains, changing purple heather to dark canyons; silver lichen-laced rock turns to black. I jump into a hollow, imagine living with the seasons, and all nature coming and going, building shelter from wind and weather, from turf and stone with hands hard as leather, eating fish, and drinking water, walking with only the wind and my shadow through the crystal air, bog and heather.

Beside the fire, the mind sings its half-century song of places and times, gone, known, changed.

This is not what is wanted, this kaleidoscope tumbling; swaying mood and emotion, like a breeze through summer grasses.

Memories, foam flecks on the sea always in motion.

Concentrate, adjust the fine focus . . . One place. One time.

Oh the shock of it, the burning, churning rot of it.
Joys that fall like stars from heaven.
Griefs that come like hurricanes; hell-driven.
Oh the mock of it, the clods, the clutter, the mess of it.
The tangled webs, the teased delights; the endless 'if onlys'.
Too quick responses . . . 'but I was right'.

The private excuses made when musing on places and times held
deep within the sunlit days, and dark nights of memory.

I will return to this . . . some other time, for now I run with the
fox and hunt with the hounds . . .
(*Jean Arbuckle, 1996*)

You could use an image from a dream, too, and explore this; or
simply the first idea or image that comes to mind. As usual with
this kind of writing practice, try not to force the writing; just
keep following the thread that suggests itself, wherever it leads,
however apparently disconnected or disjointed your writing
seems to be.

Allow your imagination to indulge itself, to play. Listen to it.
Sometimes it will want to dart and flutter, like a butterfly, flitting
from image to image, idea to idea, drawn by colour and scent, and
your writing will reflect this. On these days you may end up with
a vivid patchwork of ideas and phrases and word-pictures. Another
day your imagination will want to plumb the depths by exploring
one particular memory or image or idea or feeling in detail and at
length.

The more flexibility you can allow into your writing practice
and your writing life, the more exciting and substantial and wide-
ranging the products of your imagination will be. Don't narrow
your writing horizons by limiting yourself to one habitual mode
of expression, one style, one voice.

Writing practice

As fast as possible, write:

- ten connected sentences (continuity and development of content)
- ten totally unconnected sentences (each to have its own theme, unrelated to the rest)
- four sentences which are connected in some way, but not necessarily the most obvious way (looking for lateral thinking)

Here is an example of the latter from workshop participants:

> He pressed the frozen puddle with his fist and the ice broke into jagged shards of temporary glass.
> The July evening was still stiflingly hot but the clink of the ice in the glass was an invitingly cool sound.
> That had been the last of the set of glasses they had been given for a wedding present and now it lay shattered.
> After the wedding the ice crept in and eventually shattered their marriage like a glass dropped on a stone floor.
> (*Jenny Twomey & Stuart Hall*)

Visualization

If you want to use this visualization, you might like to record it onto a tape, allowing pauses as necessary for you to picture the scene described. Or you could ask someone to read you through it, again bearing in mind the need to read it slowly and pause. Close your eyes (except to note things down, unless your memory's good enough to save it all to record at the end).

> You are above a foreign town, on a hillside. Below you the houses cluster, clinging and tumbling down the mountainside.
> What sounds reach you up here? What smells are carried on the

breeze? What are the predominant colours surrounding you? What are the views?

Notice the time of day, and the weather. Can you feel sun, or wind, on your skin, your hair, your back?

There are rough steps cut into the hillside, leading away from the summit to the town below. You follow these until you descend into a narrow alleyway, cobbled; houses leaning close, flowers straggling over the walls and rioting in doorways and porches. It's a little darker here amongst the houses; human voices and different smells replace the ones on the hillside.

There's a flight of steps in front of you, with a handrail on the left. At the bottom of these is a horseshoe-shaped square, with a tree or fountain in the middle. You pause here a moment to look around you. At the far side of the square is a cathedral or similar building constructed from a creamy-ochre coloured stone. It attracts you and you move towards it, but as you do so you see beside it a small archway surrounded by a climbing shrub. You realize that it is the archway that you want to enter, not the building. Look carefully at it as you approach. As you get there, you notice that there is an object waiting for you to pick it up; a talisman. When you've done this, step through . . .

When you are ready, come back into the square and sit by the tree or fountain in the middle. Then open your eyes and write it all down.

You can adapt this, if you like, to picture a home or holiday setting for any of the characters in your book. When you walk through the archway, you could then invite one or more of your characters to be present, and talk with them, ask them questions.

Speaking in other voices

Good practice for the creative writer is to take on a different personality and write from that perspective from time to time. The easiest way to do this is to imagine a career which you have never considered. Then spend twenty minutes or more writing about an event or period in a day in the life of someone following that career.

Try a deep-sea diver, a bus conductor, a cosmetic surgeon, a funeral director, a groom, a courier, an Egyptian temple guide, a clairvoyant, a yoga instructor, a chef, an interpreter, a gardener, a psychiatric nurse, a guide-dog trainer, a fisherman, a crofter, a drug-smuggler, a politician, a beauty-therapist, etc. Obviously there is a temptation – or even a need – to draw on stereotypes when doing this exercise; try and be as original as possible and get inside the profession. There's scope for humour here, too.

Telling tales

If you haven't already done this, take a memory of an event in your life. What's the theme? Pare it down to the barest bones of the incident. This happened, then that happened. Give it to a fictionalized character. Now dress it up in different clothes, embroider it, create a different setting using the same theme.

New clichés

Take some stems from clichés in common usage. Discard the old ending and make up your own. For example:

- as wise as Nostradamus
- as wise as retrospection
- as cold as a turned back
- as cold as a decree nisi
- as black as a judge's nightmares
- as black as a fallen angel
- as innocent as a white petticoat
- as stiff as a Bible
- as stiff as a tulip
- as red as a dunce's copybook

6   Stories and Plots

Fact and fiction

In *Aspects of the Novel*, E.M. Forster quotes André Gide, who in *Les Faux Monnayeurs* proposes the idea that a major issue for the novelist is the struggle between what reality offers and what you try to make of that offer.

This is, I think, a fair summary of fiction writing with its peculiar blend of fantasy and reality. The novel-writing process draws primarily on three things: what you know, what you can research and what you can imagine.

For a first-time novelist, it's tempting to write autobiographically; by which I mean to attempt to create fiction out of your own life experiences. Sadly, however, autobiography on its own is not enough. Your unadulterated life experiences, in terms of plot, are more likely to yield anecdotes than stories. Of course there are exceptions to this; if, for instance, you are already a celebrity, you will possibly have a ready-made audience who think you're sufficiently interesting to guarantee sales. If you have had a particularly scandalous past, or have achieved remarkable feats like sailing round the world single-handed as a disabled granny or a sixteen-year-old, you will only have to arrange your memories or diaries into a narrative sequence. People like Brian Keenan, who've undergone such things as being taken hostage and/or tortured, will find a ready market – we all want to read about people who've been to hell and come back to tell us about it. And these books, of course, are not strictly speaking novels – they don't need to be. However, someone with that kind of experience behind him or her will have a head start on the rest of us.

But the somewhat unpalatable truth is that most of us live, to some extent or another, lives that fall somewhere between boringly mundane and fairly interesting in the high points. Who's going to read about these kinds of lives? So whilst your own life experiences may provide the skeleton of a story and insight into how people behave, they are rarely substantial enough to carry the weight of a plot or engage the excitement of a reader. You will need significant dollops of fantasy and imagined possibilities to turn life experiences into a novel.

The good news, however, is that personal experience does offer us extraordinary insights into what it means to be human. The autobiographical aspects can provide motivations, blueprints for characters, an understanding of psychological and emotional dynamics, life situations, careers and scenes. Your experiences can be drawn on to make your characters into real people and your settings into real places. This is what is meant by 'write about what you know', which on the whole is sound advice (even though not far-reaching enough on its own). Unless you have experienced it or something like it at first hand, it's hard to put yourself into the life and mind of a serial killer, a child in Rwanda, a Muslim in Bosnia, a Hollywood superstar, a Tibetan monk in exile. If you haven't been to Fiji, it might be tricky setting a book there. If you've never scaled anything more demanding than a kitchen chair to change a light-bulb, your account of a tragedy on Annapurna may not ring true. Imagination and research will of course fill in many gaps, but your strength will be in drawing on a situation of which you have some experience, or in which you can, through sufficiently similar experiences, imagine yourself.

However, we can all draw on the experience of being human; we can all practise putting ourselves in each other's shoes. We've all felt fear, excitement, boredom, awe, shame, greed and so on; if you can portray these things skilfully enough you can make up for the areas where you are having to guess and imagine.

Good research will not only give your book weight, it will also help convince your reader to read on. A reader needs to know early on that *you* know what you're talking about. This means getting your facts right. So turn your autobiography to your advantage: draw on what you know to create a believable main character, setting and life situation. The simplest way to do this for a first-time novelist is to give your main character your career, or a similar one, and plant him or her in your home town, or one you know well. You can draw on your experiences of being married, divorced, a parent, a sibling, unemployed, a football fan, a photographer, a horsewoman, a member of an ethnic group or of a particular church or society, the 'other woman', or whatever life has brought to you as well. If you're a worker in a car factory, you'll make your task as a novelist easier by drawing on this. If you're a lawyer, ditto. Of course, you may feel that this does not give you a lot of mileage; but if you know nothing about animals or medical science but make your central character into a vet, you will have an enormous amount of research to do to convince your readers.

If you're writing about crime, or prehistory, or horror or sci-fi it's likely to be impossible, or at least more difficult, to write from experience. In this case, your research needs to be impeccable and your authority and imagination need to be such that your reader is willing to be convinced by what you're saying. You will have to work harder to gain your readers' trust and acceptance, to persuade them to suspend their disbelief.

Research can take the form of background reading, interviews with people who are authorities on your subject, time spent in libraries or museums. Most people are only too happy to share information with you if you are genuinely interested, and approach them with courtesy. Keep your eyes and ears 'on call' and keep notes, including in them the source of your information in case you need to query or double-check facts. Date your notes, too, and file them where they are easily retrievable.

Be careful where you set your book. I've said elsewhere that little will lose your reader faster than setting a book in a town or country he or she knows well and you evidently don't. It's worth taking the time to get places, dates, historical events and the like as accurate as humanly possible.

So in summary, use your sources for what you know and what you can research, add a hefty dose of imagination, and hope that the muse will come along for the final alchemy.

Themes

Behind every successful novel is a theme. It may not be overt, and it may not even be conscious in the mind of the writer, but if you were to look for it, you'd find it. Often there is more than one theme, but usually one is predominant. The chances are that the theme you write on has a connection with the themes that underpin your own life. Many can be summed up in a single word: betrayal, revenge, loss, jealousy, ambition, justice, love. Others need a phrase: triumph of love over adversity, transformation through crisis, missed opportunity, mistaken identity, the inexorability of fate, one's past catching up with one, obsessive jealousy, unrequited passion, sibling rivalry, survival against all odds, life in a small community, the love triangle and so on. Often the theme centres on a conflict: the 'outsider' versus society, nomadic versus fixed lifestyles, riches versus poverty, brains against beauty, freedom versus responsibility, love versus duty. The list is as broad as human experience.

What is important to bear in mind is that the theme can be defined as the central issue, motivation or problem, in a character's life. The issue may be subtle and low-key or dramatic and all-consuming. It may be the ground of an individual's life, or it may appear suddenly as the result of an external event, such as bankruptcy or falling in love.

The creative tension inherent in the story is intimately connected with its theme. If the theme is linked with the motivations, desires and needs of the central character, as it normally is, the thwarting of those desires and motivations gives us the suspense, the tension, necessary to generate a plot, provides the crises which provide turning points and climax, and moves the story on to its inevitable conclusion. For this reason, it helps at some stage to have an awareness of your underlying theme, even if you have not chosen it consciously, and you might want to ask yourself what you want to say, what message you want to convey, with your theme. Do you have a purpose in mind? In what way do you believe that love conquers all? Are you wanting to deliver a philosophical comment on the theme of missed opportunity? What comes about as a result of your character's transformation through crisis? What changes might take place in the way he relates to his wife/family/the world? What does unrequited passion mean in the life of your protagonist? What effects does this have? All these issues kept in mind enable you to keep your writing 'on track'.

Story

There is a certain amount of public confusion about what constitutes story, and what plot. For the purposes of this book, we shall define story as follows. In its simplest interpretation, a story is the 'what' of the book: a recounting of events in narrative form, linked largely by chronology, their passage through time. 'This happened, then that happened.' Or in E.M. Forster's famous analysis, 'The king died, then the queen died.' While the theme may be summarized in a word, a phrase or a sentence, the story may be summarized in its main elements in a half-page or a page.

Plot

Plot is what adds complexity and individuality to a work of fiction. If story is the 'what' then plot is the 'why', the connecting tissue.

Plot is bound up with consequences: with cause and effect, action and reaction, human interaction and its results. This is where psychology comes in to overlay a living, dynamic fabric on the inert chassis of story. Forster again: 'The king died, then the queen died *of grief.*' This is plot. We now know why the queen died. Plot makes story three-dimensional. It combines action and emotion, event and psychology. You will see that there is potential for very sophisticated chain-reactions. The story unfolds in the way that it does because of the words and actions of the main character(s) and the effect that they have on their immediate environment, community, society and circle of family and friends (or lack of them). This in turn unfolds as it does in relation to the theme underlying the book, which is why the main character behaves as he or she does.

To relate this process to human biology, we could say that the initial idea or inspiration behind the book, the *generating spark*, is the meeting of sperm and ovum, out of which will grow the foetus. The *theme* provides the cellular blueprint; what will make this individual, this book, into what it is. The *story* is the skeleton. The *plot* is not only the flesh but the mass of veins, muscles and organs, as well as the physical and perhaps more importantly here psychological characteristics which make up the individual, human but unique. Because of its complexity, plot seems to have a life of its own, and as you write it it may evolve from your original idea into something quite different. So it's not a static fixed form but, as Ronald Tobias says, a dynamic process which saturates the book in its intricacy. Plot takes a few pages to recount, and in effect consti-tutes your synopsis. (The book itself is the 'how', showing the effects of the 'what' and the 'why' combined.)

How many possible plots are there? Various books suggest that there are innumerable plots. Aristotle tells us that there are only two: tragedy, and comedy. (These, it seems, are determined by whether an individual's main motivation is towards happiness or unhappiness.)

It has been suggested by a number of different writers that there are seven basic plots in the world – archetypal motifs which crop up in myths and stories from all parts of the world. In case this is helpful, I'll list them here:

1   The Quest (epitomized by the search for the Holy Grail; contemporary literature still draws hugely on this source – the popularity of cult books such as *Lord of the Rings* testifies to its enduring appeal)
2   The Tragic Love Story (*Romeo and Juliet, Tristan and Isolde*)
3   The Happy Ever After Against All Odds Love Story (*Cinderella, Snow White*)
4   The Hero with the Fatal Flaw (Achilles, Vulcan, Icarus, Hamlet, Macbeth)
5   Triumph of Good over Evil/Virtue Rewarded (the theme of many fairy stories; also such stories as *Star Wars*)
6   The Eternal Triangle (Arthur, Guinevere and Lancelot)
7   Nemesis/Divine Retribution – your past catching up with you (Lear, Othello, Rochester in *Jane Eyre*).

You will see for yourself how theme and plot are interlinked. It's clearly also arguable how watertight these categories are: *Star Wars* could also be seen as a Quest; Lear, Othello and Rochester could be described as flawed heroes; it could be said that Hamlet met his nemesis in death. Macbeth, too, could equally fit category seven. Is *Lord of the Rings* actually a story primarily about the triumph of good over evil? Perhaps the usefulness of a categorization system such as this is to offer you a framework and a focus.

However, regardless of how many possible plots there are in the world and whether or not you can fit your book into a pigeon-hole, your success, ultimately, will depend on how good a story-teller you are and how original your creation is. Each person's raw material is unique; a story I might write about a Quest will be utterly different from one you write – even if we both took our inspiration from the same initial source.

A practical word of warning, though; whilst categorization is a lot looser today with the advent of the 'contemporary novel', publishers still like to know where your book fits into the accepted scheme of literary genres. It's worth giving this a little thought, even if you abandon it as too much of a constraint.

Writing practice

Other people's books

Take several books with which you've been impressed, preferably in different genres or styles. Using a sheet of paper per book, copy down the jacket 'blurb'. Compare these with each other. How do they differ? Allowing for variations in publishing-house style, can you see similarities? What are the main points being made? The main emphasis? Do any or all of these books fit in to any of the above seven categories? Or do they draw on several? (This exercise has a threefold purpose: first, to accustom you to the idea of picking out salient points in a work of fiction; secondly, to give you practice in the way the blurb is constructed, which in turn will help to focus you on the main points in your own book; thirdly, to help you garner ideas.)

What is the theme in each book? If pared down to its bones, does it fit a simple storyline such as 'boy meets girl, boy loses girl, boy gets girl back'? Do the books have themes in common?

In your own words and without referring to the blurb, summarize the plot of each book.

Now take another book you have read.

1 Define the central character's problem.
2 Define the motivation of this character. How does it relate to the problem?
3 Say what the major conflicts and turning points are. How are they related to each other, to the theme and to the central issue?

Your raw material

List:

- where you have lived
- where you have travelled
- what you know about
- what you have studied
- what you have done out of the ordinary
- what adjectives apply to your experience of family/love/work/ community
- what the big events have been in your life

Now give this event to a different character in a slightly different set of circumstances, dramatizing it. Write in the present tense, again, but in the third person.

Your novel

- What kind of story do you want to write/are you writing?
- Whose story is it (who is the right central character for this story)?
- What was the originating idea?
- What is its basic theme – in one word if possible?
- What is its plot in just two or three sentences
- What is its book-jacket blurb – in fifty words?
- What is its working title?

7   Characterization

Real people or cardboard cutouts?

Fundamentally, there are three things that will ensure that a reader or publisher turns over to continue reading at the bottom of page one. One is the promise of an intriguing plot; in this I include a good opening paragraph. Another is an original and fresh writing style that is nonetheless undemanding. The third is one or more characters to whom the reader feels an attraction, or who at least are capable of engaging interest.

With few exceptions, novels are first and foremost about people; about their experiences, their emotions, their mistakes and triumphs, terrors and glories, challenges and changes. The situations may be exaggerated, the characters larger than life, but they must echo real life, and the real dilemmas and problems real people face.

What we tend to remember most about a book that has caught our imagination are the main characters. What's more, a glance at bestsellers will reveal strong, well-created central characters with credible motivations, strength of purpose and the will-power, faith or energy to face and hopefully overcome conflict and difficulties. A book's success has much to do with the ability of an author to create such characters.

Aspiring authors sometimes ask about using real people and actual situations as 'templates' for fictional characters. There are of course advantages and disadvantages to doing this. While it's helpful to use isolated characteristics from a number of people to create a kind of composite character, it may work against you if you draw extensively on people you know as material for your books – it can make enemies out of erstwhile friends through hurt or offended feelings, no matter how carefully you try to portray your characters. The same goes for borrowing names or careers and also life situations, particularly tragic ones.

However, careful observation of other people's lives is crucial if your characters are to come alive, to be substantial and believable, three-dimensional. There is no substitute. What do you do? Perhaps the best advice is to beware of the temptation to draw on material or people too close to home, and to change major characteristics when drawing on real personalities or events. Above all, tread with sensitivity and be a little judicious. If your best friend's mother died of cancer and you were with her throughout the process, it may not be wise to make use of this in a similar situation in your next book. On the other hand, a description of a sailing accident which happened to a friend of a friend of a friend a number of years ago is unlikely to cause offence when recycled later in a fourth-hand and adapted fictional form.

Readers don't necessarily need to like your characters, but they do need to be able to believe in them, and we do need them to engage our interest and our sympathy,.

Have a look at how E. Annie Proulx shows us her main character, Quoyle, in *The Shipping News*.

The book opens with an unremarkable and rather downbeat first line: 'Here is an account of a few years in the life of Quoyle, born in Brooklyn and raised in a shuffle of dreary upstate towns.'

The next paragraph – the second sentence of the book – engages our interest, and introduces Quoyle: 'Hive-spangled, gut roaring with gas and cramp, he survived childhood; at the state university, hand clapped over his chin, he camouflaged torment with smiles and silence. Stumbled through his twenties and into his thirties learning to separate his feelings from his life, counting on nothing. He ate prodigiously, liked a ham knuckle, buttered spuds.'

This paragraph leaves us intrigued, with a number of questions. What was his childhood like? What torment was he hiding with his hand clapped to his chin? What happened to him that made him separate his feelings from his life, that left him feeling that nothing (and presumably nobody) could be trusted? We learn that he had an appetite for conservative and fattening food; that he seemed inept ('stumbled through his twenties . . .'), possibly shy and lonely, possibly shunned or spurned.

Over the next two pages the portrait of Quoyle is developed. We learn that he was teased and bullied, that he hated and feared water; that he could make sense of nothing, that at university he took courses he didn't understand, that he 'humped back and forth' speaking to no one, that he went home 'for weekends of excoriation'.

Proulx gives us a physical portrait, too: Quoyle's chief failure was

a failure of normal appearance . . . Quoyle shambled, a head taller than any child around him, was soft . . . A great damp loaf of a body . . . At sixteen he was buried under a casement of flesh. Head shaped like a crenshaw, no neck, reddish hair ruched back. Features as bunched as kissed fingertips. Eyes the colour of plastic. A monstrous chin, a freakish shelf jutting from the lower face.

As a child, the author tells us, the character 'invented stratagems to deflect stares; a smile, a downcast gaze, the right hand darting up to cover the chin.'

Simultaneously with conjuring a picture of Quoyle as physically unappealing, Proulx manages to ensure that our sympathy is engaged. She tells us that Quoyle 'was a failure at loneliness, yearned to be gregarious, to know his company was a pleasure to others'. With this, she brings into play one of the most basic of human needs: that of belonging. She successfully treads the narrow path between a character so unattractive he doesn't interest us and one so pathetic that we are irritated by his weaknesses. Her protagonist is not, somehow, a fat, repulsive self-indulgent slob who does not move us; he is rather a sensitive, alienated, misunderstood misfit who is the butt of societal or familial taunts and misfortune. We all have our weak spots, our Achilles' heel; we all wish secretly to see the underdog make good. We want to know how he will overcome these adversities. What's more, we now have a good idea as to Quoyle's central problem, the underlying potential in the book for conflict.

Proulx's flair for characterization continues through the novel. In the next short passage, on page four, we're given a brief glimpse of other characters; the contrast between the three characters serves to emphasize and deepen our picture of Quoyle.

> Their differences: Partridge black, small, a restless traveller across the slope of life, an all-night talker; Mercalia, second wife of Partridge and the colour of a brown feather on dark water, a hot intelligence; Quoyle, large, white, stumbling along, going nowhere.
>
> Partridge saw beyond the present, got quick shots of coming events as though loose brain wires briefly connected . . . He could blow perfect smoke rings. Cedar waxwings always stopped in his yard on their migration flights.
>
> Ed Punch talked out of the middle of his mouth.

The last sentence is a good example of 'instant characterization'. It will help you as author as well as the reader if you can introduce personality quirks which enable us to conjure a picture of a character. When putting together your character portrait as suggested at the end of this chapter, try and include these kinds of idiosyncrasies. Partridge blows perfect smoke rings. Ed Punch talks out of the middle of his mouth. Quoyle covers his chin with his hand. We remember these details; these are real people, convincing people, even when they may echo certain stereotypes.

Living characters

As a novelist, you need to be able to convince a reader that you are portraying real people. You need to be able to bring them alive, to show them in relation to their world and to each other, with flesh-and-blood reactions, words and deeds.

A general rule of thumb – which actually Proulx breaks in some of the examples above – is the usual 'show, not tell' (there are of course occasions when for reasons of speed or space you will opt to tell us certain things about your character). On the whole, rather than giving your reader factual descriptions, allow the character to unfold through his or her actions and relationships. We can learn about a character through their past and present actions, through their dreams and aspirations, through what they do and how and why, through what they say, how they say it and what they think, through the reactions of other people to them, through what other characters in the book have to say about them, and through their relationships, habits, hobbies, opinions, attitudes, beliefs, politics. Above all, show a reader your character's motives, remember that in fiction, as in fact, motivations may often be contradictory.

The key word in building character, perhaps, is 'relationships' – whether this is to themselves, their friends, family, community or the wider world. It's vital to remember that your character is not acting in a void; that his or her constructed world includes other people and a whole network of actions and chain-reactions. Nothing happens in a void, in fiction any more than in real life. How your character relates to the world and the other people in it has a bearing on the success of your novel. Show this through the other characters and the plot development within the book, rather than by telling your reader as an author. 'One of the reasons why bad novels are bad,' said Sir Victor Pritchett (the *Guardian*, 22 March 1997), 'is not that the characters do not live, but that they do not live with each other. They read one another's minds through the author.'

Caring about your characters

An important aspect of character portrayal is Forster's concept of interior life; you will remember that he suggested that one of the reasons for reading fiction is to have access to the normally hidden 'secret lives' of people. If you are able to show this inner life your characters will take on a depth, a vitality, a vibrancy and substance which will allow them to remain in a reader's mind long after the book is finished. A character in a book which achieves this is, for a reader, almost like meeting a new friend.

A novelist can do this by writing in a way which reveals the characters' emotions and thoughts, inner responses. Novelist Pauline Bentley suggests that an author immerse him- or herself in the main character's mind as each scene is enacted in order to write it with maximum impact.

You as author must care about your characters. You need to be emotionally involved with them, even when, as happens in real life, they're not always likeable. You must have an emotional investment in what happens to them and how they handle it (or don't). You must be able to perceive and show them as unique individuals with their own agendas, sets of beliefs, habits and opinions, quirks and foibles. You must want to know all about them, as you would a close friend or a lover. If you do, then there is a good chance you will pass this involvement on to your reader. Forster proposes that, for a reader, a character becomes real once it is obvious that the author knows everything about him or her; which is, as I've suggested already, a privilege which perhaps only a novelist, and through the novelist a reader, may have *vis à vis* another human being.

In summary, then, the first requirement for a novelist is that you care about your characters to the extent of being passionately involved in their lives; and in so doing, draw out of them the necessary aspects of their inner lives; as well as being able to portray their outer ones. (As with everything else, it's important to keep the sense of 'interior life' in proportion, of course. Balance introspection or reflective passages with action.)

The second requirement is that the author is capable of a certain amount of artistic detachment. Without this, you are in danger of being swallowed by the characters to the extent that the plot starts to ramble and objective perspective is sacrificed. You need still to be able to gauge what works and what doesn't, and to be able to intervene once the characters have come alive to the extent that they start to hijack the book – which does happen, as any novelist will tell you. This is a double-edged sword; simultaneously proof that the characters work and advance warning of a possible coup, a mutiny. The novelist has to remain focused enough on the purpose behind the novel and the desired outcome of the plot to remain at least partly unmoved by the new directions that suggest themselves as a result of the interaction between characters, and between characters and material. At the same time, the new ideas may offer helpful twists and unexpected angles or depths; if you can remain both objective and flexible, you will be able to see more clearly whether and where these might fit.

A novelist needs to learn to differentiate between the times when he or she needs to 'light the touchpaper and stand back' (to allow the dynamics created by the development of the characters and the plot to come into play as they would in real life), and when he or she needs to have firm hold of the reins.

Main/major/minor characters

Characters in a novel can be seen as foreground or background. Main and major characters fit into the former category; in the latter belong minor characters and those whose rôles are closer to those of sets or props.

Most novels have just one or two main characters around whom the story revolves. These protagonists are largely responsible for the success or otherwise of the book. Most of the action takes place through their eyes; we see the story from their perspective. The protagonists need to be at the heart of the plot, in the forefront of events as much as possible. These are the ones on whose history, present circumstances and psychology you cannot afford to skimp. That doesn't mean that your book will be laden with all that information; but you as novelist need to have as complete a picture of them and their lives as possible. It's unwise, incidentally, to have more than three main characters until you are confident of your fiction writing ability, as you risk diluting the impact of character and plot.

Major characters are sufficiently well developed as to come across as real people, but are less important and therefore less whole, or rounded, than your main protagonist(s). They serve to shed further light on your protagonist and to move the story forward. They are central enough to the story to influence the major events in the book, but we do not have the same access to their lives, especially their thoughts and feelings, as we do to the protagonists. However, a reader needs to be made to care about what happens to these characters – good or bad – too. Once again, they don't have to like them, but they do have to be engaged with them.

The 'background' characters are of two sorts. There are the ones who are incidentally important to the plot, such as the ex-wife whom we never meet but who continues to thwart the protagonist in his aims; or, for example, the truck driver in *The Horse Whisperer* who in killing a horse and rider sets in motion the whole story. There might be an elderly father-in-law who lives in, or an absent teenage daughter whose drug problems affect the whole family. Minor characters such as these can also shed light on the protagonist as they offer opportunities to illustrate the protagonist's qualities or idiosyncrasies. (How does your heroine relate to the elderly father-in-law? What does the new lover's reaction to the teenage daughter say about him?) These people may be indirectly instrumental to the plot but do not necessarily put in frequent appearances. As they represent something – a cause, a problem, family ties and the like – their rôle is more important, in a way, than their characterization.

Then there are the background characters who exist to portray 'real life' – the neighbour, the schoolteacher, the bus driver, the colleague, the publican, the local shopkeeper. These are what

Forster defined as 'flat' characters – they do not need to be developed as people; often they are stereotyped. In a way they are a canvas against which the identifying characteristics of the major characters are little by little painted in.

Names

Names are important. Names tell us a lot about someone – whether we're conscious of it or not, we all react to a name, according to our personal and social associations with it. Certain names call to mind certain social groupings. What are your own associations with Cynthia Buckley-Bowler? Piers Hestlethwaite? Darren Jones? Kevin Murphy? Sharon Smith? Jake Blacker? How do you respond to Sinead O'Sullivan or Carlos Manuel Ortega? And age – naming your heroine Iris or Agnes or Hilda or Phyllis will give a different impression of age and era to a reader than Jo or Holly or Sam or Cass. Is your hero a Daniel, a Leo, a Tristan or a Joseph? Or a Philip, Richard, Iain or Jack? A Sean or a Jason? Does he have middle names? Is it significant that he does or doesn't?

Names of course also tell us something about the parents. Is your character's background likely to be conventional or unusual?

If you have settled on names, it's worth considering the connotations they may hold for a reader.

Character construction by numbers

This is really by way of a note of caution. At the end of this chapter you will find an exercise which will act as a fact file for your characters. This 'template' is one of the most useful tools you can have for starting to create a character, getting a 'feel' for their physical, emotional, social and financial circumstances.

However, to turn these two-dimensional shadowy figures into

believable people, it's vital that you reflect on what the characteristics and circumstances that you're recording might mean in terms
of your characters' lives. If your main character was born in
Brooklyn to poor immigrants who put him up immediately for
adoption, what might this mean in terms of his subsequent attitudes, difficulties and achievements? How would these differ from
the expectations, attitudes and experiences of the sixth daughter of
rural Irish farmers travelling to London for the first time to find
work? Or the privileged only son of elderly wealthy landowners
who is mercilessly bullied throughout his public-school years?

Think of Quoyle: his hinted-at unhappy childhood, his fat,
lumpish body, his shelf-like chin. It's no surprise when we learn
that he's lonely, lacking in all confidence and sparkle, thinks of
himself as a loser, expecting, somehow, misery and taunting. There
is a coherence and congruence in the facts that we're given and the
attributes connected with them.

Constructing a character is about so much more than merely
listing arbitrary facts about them. It can help, particularly in terms
of psychological insights into your characters, to take a lateral
angle. You could try that party game: 'if s/he were a vehicle/piece
of furniture/animal, what might s/he be?'

Viewpoint

Viewpoint is tricky. You need to know whose story you're telling,
and just how many perspectives you can use without diluting the
book and losing your readers' interest because they are unable to
relate in depth to any of your characters. It helps to be clear about
this from the outset; many new writers stumble with this one, and
weaken their novel because of it. David Lodge, in his book *The Art
of Fiction*, says that viewpoint is perhaps the most important single
decision the novelist will make. Choice of viewpoint, he continues, determines a reader's emotional and moral response to the
characters and their actions and dilemmas. For example, how

differently would we react to *Jane Eyre* if the story was narrated by the mad locked-away wife? Or by Rebecca herself in Daphne du Maurier's book of the same name?

Of course in 'real life' an event is likely to be experienced, or at least witnessed, by more than one person. One of the strengths of the novel is that it can portray different experiences or perceptions of the same event from different viewpoints, though clearly only one at a time; and there is a price you pay for this. One of the differences, for instance, between fiction and factual reportage such as journalism or history is that in the latter the recorder is an impartial observer who, in order to give a clear, objective report will draw on all relevant participants for a rounded picture. The result is a detailed picture but little facility for a reader to get inside the life and mind of one of the individuals. Subsequently, it's harder to really care about what happens to them. In this kind of 'flat' writing, what works for non-fiction will not work for fiction.

This may be the case in what's known as the 'omniscient' narrative method, where the action is reported from a god's-eye view. In this narrative style, you move from person to person, place to place, dipping in and out of events and actions. As narrator, you can explain to the reader exactly what's going on with whomever you want. This perhaps gives the greatest freedom of the three most common narrative 'voices'. It allows the jigsaw to be built up more quickly than either the limited third-person narration or the first person. As a device it can also be effectively used to build suspense – switching perspectives at the interesting moment (though it can also be frustrating beyond belief to read), especially to heighten tension at the climax, and to show the reader important pieces of information which may be hidden from the other characters. Nicholas Evans in *The Horse Whisperer* uses this device in the dramatic opening chapter of his book, where we switch from the teenagers Grace and Judith going riding into the snowy morning, to Wayne the truck driver, to Grace's mother Annie, back again to Wayne/Grace/Wayne, Grace/Judith/Wayne in the accident scene, Robert, Grace's father, then the post-accident scene and its attendants, then Annie again, all within thirty-one pages. The next chapter switches viewpoints a number of times, and then slowly the book settles down to a more limited third-person narration, focusing largely on the four main characters: Annie, Grace, Tom the Whisperer and Robert (and Pilgrim the horse).

Omniscient third-person narration can work well in action books, humorous books and novels which cover large spans of space or time and a number of characters, where reader involvement with the characters is less important than the story.

The three significant drawbacks of omniscient narration are: first, that there's a danger that the narrative will start to ramble, that the novelist will lose the focus; secondly, the authorial intrusion – God-like pronouncements from above as a kind of running commentary – will break the flow and disrupt credibility; and thirdly, that the reader will be viewing the story from afar rather than becoming emotionally involved. Inevitably, a reader will notice the narrator more, although in some styles – such as comic writing – this could be turned to your advantage.

Limited third-person narration is the most common, the easiest and arguably the most effective form of storytelling. In omniscient viewpoint, we see events and people as the *narrator* sees them. In limited third-person we see them as the *character* sees or experiences them. In this viewpoint we are allowed a deeper, more intense involvement with the characters; we can identify with them, feel with them. We, the author or readers, are drawn through the story by one (or two or three) people only. Whilst in omniscient viewpoint the author/narrator switches viewpoint at will, with limited third-person narration the viewpoint will change, if at all, much less often, and this will normally occur at a chapter-break or possibly a scene-break. During the time when we are with one character, we can only be aware of what is going on inside that character's mind; even though we are using the third person, 'he' or 'she', we see as if through their eyes for that chapter or scene. While we are following the thread of that character's story, we do not have access to the thoughts of other characters except through what they tell us (by 'us' I mean the character from whose viewpoint we're narrating, as well as the reader) or what the viewpoint character guesses or deduces. However, if you, as author, choose, you can still step back to some degree and 'pan' other events and perspectives to set a scene, to introduce other characters, to show us a crucial incident happening out of sight of the main character, or switch to the viewpoint of a *limited* number of other main characters. The important thing to be aware of is the possible effect of 'distancing' on a reader, if you do this too often.

First-person narrative is an increasingly common perspective, with equally weighted advocates and opponents. Of the three options it clearly allows the most intense involvement between reader and character. Climbing inside a character's head gives us the deepest possible emotional engagement with that character. It's also perhaps the most natural choice for a beginning writer, as it feels comfortable and allows you to really 'think' yourself into a character. It is possible to switch between separate first-person viewpoints in your book (in separate chapters preferably), but at the risk of losing your reader's sympathy or attention. The effort involved in creating two or more sufficiently different and distinctive voices in the first person also puts heavy demands on the author.

The downside of first-person narration is twofold. The first aspect is that your vision is very limited – you *only* have access to that person's thoughts and feelings throughout the book; only the incidents and events at which he or she was present or about which we witness him or her being told. Everything has to be filtered through what it is physically possible for that person to have witnessed or experienced. Connected with this is the second aspect, which is that for some reason most beginning novelists completely overlook this, despite the fact that it's our own perspective in real life! So the message is, use first person if that's what you want to do, but beware of mistakes like: 'I'd been watching Helen all evening. She'd been looking kind of upset. Around about eleven I went over and asked her if she'd like me to walk her home. I was nervous; my hand shook and I nearly spilt my beer down her front. Helen looked at the slopping beer, looked back at me. She was wondering what to say that wouldn't be offensive; deep down, she thought I was a jerk.' How do you *know* this? The only way this would work would be to rephrase it thus: 'Helen looked at me. I was afraid that she'd think I was a jerk. The next moment she blurted out: "I don't want to offend you, but . . ." ' The ones to watch for, of course, are often more subtle than this, where you forget that the viewpoint character doesn't necessarily have access to all the information that you do about, for instance, the future or other characters.

So the choice is yours to make wisely, as fits your book and style.

Show, not tell

A common mistake with beginning novelists is to recount the whole story in narrative form. Two hundred pages of this is, I'm afraid, unmitigatedly dull to read, on the whole.

Is it laziness on the part of the writer? Is it fear? Whatever the reason, a reader's attention will inevitably wander, no matter how good the story, if large chunks of indigestible narrative are not broken with a change in tempo through dialogue or scene-setting.

Some authors seem to have an instinctive knack for scene-setting and dialogue; others acquire it through practice. Equally important is timing – the balance of narration with scenes; we'll look at this in chapter nine.

What the dictum 'show not tell' basically means is *let the characters do the work for you.* Rather than recounting how this happened and then that happened *show* us the event unfolding in front of our eyes, as if it were taking place on a stage. Better than telling us that Ellen had a difficult experience as a child which meant that she grew up timid and frightened of the dark and unwilling even to take a bus on her own, is to show us direct examples of Ellen's timidity in action. If necessary, appropriate and possible, give us a flashback to the original 'difficult experience'. If Mark and Joanna have a row which results in Joanna storming off and having an accident, let us hear the row and see her storming off. Make the most of the opportunity. Nicholas Evans could have told us that there had been an accident in which Judith and Judith's horse were killed and Grace and Pilgrim injured, and then got on with the rest of the story, which concerns the search for healing. Had he done so, however, he would have lost the book's major opportunity for dramatic impact, and there would be no chance for us to react to the scene and engage with the characters. It's unlikely, too, that the book would have made the bestseller list.

Having said that, it is not every scene which needs to be played out in glorious Technicolor in front of our eyes. We don't need a blow-by-blow account of Martin's interaction with the milkman – unless there is something in this exchange which is crucial for the development of the plot, which moves the story on in some way.

So don't make a scene for the sake of it. Make a scene out of something when that something is important, and when its vitality would otherwise be lost.

Is your heart in it?

Your reader needs to know that you believe in what you're writing, that you're interested in your characters and their story.

There are writers who can churn out great stories, one after the other, and admit that their motivation is the money (and it isn't by any means easy to turn out good stories and be paid for it). There are others who write what they write 'for fun' – I suspect Jilly Cooper falls into the latter category (or even both, I don't know).

But generally speaking, it's a lot easier if you can really believe in what you're writing, and write it because you really want to. This of course raises the eternal question: do you write to please yourself, or do you write to please your audience or market? Perhaps there are no black and white answers. Certainly if you want to be published there are likely to be compromises which you will need to make. Only you will know to what extent you can make them; but if the cost is that you cannot really care about the characters you are creating, it may be too high a price to pay. For the time that you're writing the book, the lives of these characters need to be almost as important to you as the lives of your family; if they're not, a reader is going to perceive them as colourless, faceless shadows. If, in your writing, you find yourself bored or impatient with a character, especially a central character, you may need to question whether this is the right character for your plot, and to find the courage to rewrite if necessary.

At the other end of the spectrum is the character with whose life you are so deeply entangled that 'real' life, at the end of the novel, feels insipid and empty. The only solution here, of course, is to start another book.

Writing practice

Write a thumbnail sketch of someone (a real person) you love, or have loved. Include a wide range of details. What's his shoe size? What makes her angry? What's his favourite expression? Favourite breakfast? Favourite book? What's he afraid of? What's her deepest desire?

List the characters in your book, from main to major to minor-important and minor-incidental if you know them. Expand a little on their situations, personalities and looks. Allow a paragraph at least for all but the most minor characters; see if you can find an identifying characteristic or two for the main and major ones.

Creating a character worksheet

This 'template' can be used for each of the main characters in your book. Try and answer the questions as fast as possible, from your intuition. As you create a physical presence for the person, you will find that the more abstract questions become easier to answer. Don't deliberate too much – just respond. Read the following three paragraphs, and then close your eyes and try to picture the answers to the questions that follow.

In your mind, picture a face. If you already know what your main character looks like, let it be this face. Otherwise, just let a face come to you – any face; don't force it, just let it form itself. It may be someone you have seen in the flesh, or it may be imaginary. If it's someone you know well, you may need to dismiss it and let another one appear.

When you have it, start to pay attention to the features: overall shape, shape and size of nose, colour and set of eyes, hair colour, skin tone and texture, facial hair or lack of it, shape of eyebrows, cheekbones, mouth, expression in mouth and eyes, moles, warts, freckles, wrinkles. When the face is clear in your imagination, note it all down as fast as possible, keeping the picture in mind.

Now add a body, with details of height, figure, size, posture, size and shape of hands and feet. Clothe that body, remembering accessories such as jewellery and shoes. What colours does this person like to wear? What is his or her voice like? Does he or she speak slowly or fast? Voluble or reticent? Impulsive or thoughtful in speech? Any idiosyncrasies? Any phrases or words he or she uses a lot? Is he or she warm or reserved?

Now jot down spontaneous answers to these questions:

- How does the character move?
- What is his or her name?
- How old is he or she?
- Married or not?
- What family?
- What job?
- Good income or struggling?
- Many or few friends?
- What are his or her interests?

- Where was he or she born and brought up?
- Town or country person?
- Night or day person?
- How does he or she relate to solitude? To crowds? To animals? To children?
- What paper does he or she read? What kind of books?
- What music?
- Favourite food? Favourite country? Favourite weather?
- What moves him or her?
- What makes him or her angry?
- Where is he or she most at peace? Most alive?
- Where and how would he or she holiday?
- What's his or her biggest weakness?
- Deepest secret?
- Most important life event to date?
- Has he or she a turbulent or stable past?
- If there could be one thing he or she could change about life so far, what would it be?
- What is his or her deepest and most secret desire?
- Biggest fear?
- What thrills him or her?
- Whom does he or she love?
- Any enemies?
- Favourite item of clothing?
- Most frequent environment?
- How does he or she envisage life in ten years' time? Any particular ambition?
- What dreams does he or she have? With whom does he or she share them?
- Earliest memory?
- Main concerns at this point in life?
- Give two random facts about this person.
- What is his or her temperament (pragmatic, phlegmatic, wary, boisterous, romantic, easygoing, extrovert, placid, volatile etc.)?
- Reaction under stress?

- Political and religious views?
- General relationships – to self, partner/spouse, family, friends, world?
- Briefly describe his or her home and location.

Finally, sum up this character's childhood. If you want to expand on this, it may be helpful to create one or two dramatic childhood events which may have a bearing on the way your character relates to the world.

8 Beginnings, Middles and Endings

Decisions made

It's self-evident, perhaps, that there are as many different approaches to writing a novel as there are writers. Chapter three explored some of these. Each person will have his or her own unique approach; for one person, it's enough to have merely the seed of an idea in mind; the book will write itself as characters develop and start to suggest their own stories. Another person might have a detailed outline summarized in skeleton or synopsis form which might run to many thousands of words, and only needs to be fleshed out to be 'the real thing'.

For most people, though, the truth lies somewhere in between. It's easier to begin once you have an idea of the starring and supporting cast of characters, a storyline and a setting. We've looked, too, at the choices to be made regarding viewpoint.

Whatever approach you take, however, most writers will agree that you need to have an idea of how your book is to end. This gives you a focus, and a means of ensuring – hopefully – that the book is not merely one long incoherent ramble (unless, of course, this is your intention), that there is some kind of order and purpose to the story you are telling. (It should be noted here that while there are some skilled writers creating lyrical and beautiful literary and experimental novels which are not plot-based, this book assumes that you are intending to follow a more traditional path.)

We've looked at creating a character. From this fairly detailed portrait you should have a clear idea of your character's background, life situation, temperament and motivations.

Four questions that need asking early on are: what is my main character's major goal? What are the main dilemmas and conflicts in my character's life which will thwart this goal or purpose? How will they show up and what will precipitate the major crisis/climax? Given all this, what is the inevitable (albeit perhaps surprising) conclusion of my book?

It often happens that the ending changes as you write the book and discover new possibilities or the characters' own developments throw in divergent and inspired, if unanticipated, circumstances. The importance of having an ending in mind at the outset is not altered by this fact, however. Allow yourself flexibility whilst still aiming to keep a sense of direction. It's rather like using a compass: whilst your general overall aim might be north, as long as you know where that lies in relation to your current position, you can choose whether to take the direct route or follow the more circuitous but appealing track through the wooded valleys or alongside the river.

The importance of conflict

Whether we like it or not, life is a series of conflicts. How we meet these conflicts – aggressively head-on, courageously standing our ground, side-stepping, fleeing – will determine to a large extent what happens next. Our conflict may be outer – with, or rather against, a person, a society, a dangerous situation – or it may be inner. In the latter case we may be struggling to reconcile opposing impulses or feelings, we may be stuck in a moral dilemma or we may have important life decisions to make which will affect others as well as ourselves.

The only way we can avoid situations of conflict is by ensuring that we live alone in a hermetically sealed environment with all our needs met without our ever having to encounter other people or hardship of any kind. Sounds impossible? It is. Besides, if this were the case there'd be no story to tell. Sad as it may be, happy people, as writer and tutor Dianne Doubtfire remarked, do not make good story material. We want to see other people go through hell fire and survive – it gives us both pleasure and hope. Or perhaps we want to see them go through hell fire and perish – getting their 'comeuppance'. We want to suffer with them, meet danger with them, love with them, laugh with them, see them get their dues. We want to *learn* from them – one of the two major reasons, I suspect, for reading a book in the first place (the other is for entertainment).

The climax or major turning point of your book is likely to be founded on a crisis, which in itself can be seen to be the inevitable outcome of a series of conflicts, each in some way linked to the others and leading inexorably to this point. Like the ending, this climax needs to be held in mind as you write, rather like a waymark (to continue the travelling analogy).

A question of balance

Writing a novel requires a blend of skills. Four of these are: a vivid imagination; a good memory and a willingness to relive, through this, some of your experiences; the ability to empathize; and an eye for detail. In addition, you need to be comfortable with and preferably excited by language, and the ability to communicate.

The need for imagination is self-evident. I suggest also a good memory because, no matter how far away from autobiography your novel is supposed to be, your own life experiences will automatically colour your writing – as indeed they should. If you're writing about people and emotions, your words will have greater impact and weight if you are able to draw on emotions you have yourself experienced. The same goes for empathy – the ability to put oneself in someone else's shoes is a crucial tool for a writer; it's part of the key to successful communication and writing which engages a reader.

Ideally, a novelist will have, or will choose to develop, a painter's eye as well as a poet's ear. This means cultivating the art of really looking and really listening; the human tendency is to see or hear what we're expecting to see or hear and screen out the rest. A writer needs to be able to look at the world afresh moment by moment, looking into what it *really* is. The best novelist will translate for a reader the impressions thus gathered in order to create a world on paper. There is something very satisfying and complete about a novel in which the author has created for us a landscape that is so real that we could walk into it, or a setting in which we can hear the creak of shoe leather or smell spring soil, smoky bars or salt air. The exercises in chapters four and five will help encourage the development of this skill.

One of the choices a novelist will face is to do with pace – a question of balance. There needs to be enough action to hold the interest, yet enough detail for a reader to be able to picture the characters, their motivations and their setting. Too much action with no let-up will exhaust a reader – a banquet needs a certain amount of moderation either side of it to be appreciated. Readers become impatient with characters whose lives appear to be constructed only of crises, with no breathing spaces. The other danger, too, of an action-packed novel is that there is no room to set scenes or allow a character to unfold as the reader gets to know him or her, and it can appear as if all the action takes place in a vacuum.

Equally unbalanced is a book which pays too much attention to detailed descriptions, with very little action to vary the pace.

As a general rule, allow a lull in the form of a chapter or part-chapter or a few pages in between dramatic scenes, as long as to do so will not dilute the previous action or impede the forward movement of the plot. (An exception to this rule might be in the build-up to the climax of the book, which may require action following swiftly on action in order to heighten the creative tension to the peak of the book.) These lulls are not empty – they can be used to deepen character-portraits or offer sub-plots as well as to paint in details and explore relationships. It's rather like the valuable eye exercises which were fashionable at one time – varying close work with practising far vision strengthens the eye-muscles. Psychologically, we do better if our close attention to the dramatic close-up of a gripping plot is relaxed now and then to look at the wider picture. What's more, this gripping and relaxing of the reader's attention is a very good device for maintaining suspense – this is after all how the cliffhanger works, bringing us to the edge of our seats and then closing the chapter. (Especially cruel, but effective in terms of sustaining the suspense, is the technique of switching scenes at the beginning of the next chapter, so that our need to know the outcome of the cliffhanger scene is intensified by having to wait.) Natural rhythms are cyclical – periods of doing followed by periods of being. Bear this in mind as you write your scenes.

Reading tastes change. A century ago writers like Dickens and Hardy would spend several pages in detailed description of a place or a person. The twentieth-century reading public on the whole does not have the patience to sit through this – society has changed and our expectations and tastes with it. In the 1950s, 1960s and 1970s, the plot-driven novel took centre stage, and considerations of setting and character development became secondary. Over the last ten or fifteen years things have started to change again, and while there will always be a market for the 'action book', more and more people are wanting to read – and write – books where character-development is the primary focus. In my opinion, how people change and how people survive will always be matters of interest, if not serious concern, to a reader; your job as novelist is to portray 'real' people in 'real' settings and believable situations (within the terms of the book; a science fiction or fantasy novel will require a different reader approach – and the appropriate suspension of disbelief – from a so-called Aga-saga, for instance.)

Whatever your genre and focus, you need to show early on that you are capable of creating characters about whom readers can care, in whom they'll be interested, in situations which they can picture and which are believable. This is all much easier if you yourself care about your characters and believe, at least for the moment, in the fiction which you are creating.

Choosing a strong opening

So far in this chapter we've looked at the general background – the wide picture. It is time to follow my own advice and look in close-up detail, starting at the beginning.

A story, by definition, requires a beginning, a middle and an end. A skilled novelist will weave these together seamlessly, so that the forward development seems natural, and indeed inevitable. Objectively examined, however, the three sections have distinct functions. The beginning introduces us to the characters and the story, the middle develops the action, and the end resolves one way or another the problems posed by the major crisis or climax. We could summarize it according to Aristotle: the beginning shows the complication, the middle the crisis, the end the solution.

The beginning could be said to be the most important piece of writing in the novel. A reader – or an editor or publisher – is likely to make the decision whether or not to continue reading based on whether you have managed to engage their interest in the first page. It's worth taking the time to get it right. Having said that, as with the ending, the beginning may change as you write the book. It's important, too, that the beginning is not overworked – by which I mean that spontaneity is not squeezed out by the zeal of 'getting it right' at all costs.

A strong opening is vital. Two cautions, though: the first is that it shouldn't be contrived purely to grip the reader's attention – beware the dramatic red herring; and the second is that the stronger and more demanding the opening, the more you'll have to live up to, as it were, in the rest of the book. Be careful, too, not to betray in Technicolor detail the end of the book in the beginning; although circular 'end-in-the-beginning' books can work very well, if too much is given away the reader has no incentive to continue reading.

Probably every creative writing tutor says the same thing: 'Begin in the middle of the action' (*in medias res*). This means deciding at which moment – preferably a reasonably dramatic one – the story actually starts, and creating a scene from this. Good ways in are questions and dialogues. Don't spend too long describing the setting or exploring the characters' histories – this can all be done later on. For the moment, the important thing is to give us only enough detail to enable us to understand what's going on, and enough action to engage our curiosity.

By the end of the first couple of pages readers should know who the main character is, have an idea of the kind of story being told and an insight into the immediate life situation of the protagonist. By the end of the first chapter they should have an idea – albeit unconsciously – of the shape of the main character's central 'problem' or dilemma. If the first chapter introduces other main characters and offers settings, moods and contexts, so much the better, as long as the story is not cluttered and diluted by these, or the reader confused.

Opening lines

Have a look at these classic opening sentences – all of them are included in the 1997 list of the top forty openings compiled (from computer analysis of the number of times they appear quoted by other people) by Oxford University Press.

1 It was a bright cold day in April, and the clocks were striking thirteen. (Orwell)
2 All happy families resemble one another, but each unhappy family is unhappy in its own way. (Tolstoy)

3 The past is a foreign country: they do things differently there. (Hartley)

4 'Take my camel, dear,' said my aunt Dot, as she climbed down from this animal on her return from High Mass. (Macaulay)

5 Mother died today. Or perhaps it was yesterday, I don't know. (Camus)

6 When Gregor Samsa awoke one morning from uneasy dreams he found himself transformed in his bed into a gigantic insect. (Kafka)

Each of these sentences sets a particular tone and its associated expectations; each offers us insight into the kind of book we have picked up; each offers us the bait of intrigue. Here's the opening line of *The Horse Whisperer* by Nicholas Evans: 'There was death at its beginning as there would be death again at its end.'

Contrast the questions we are left with in all of these openings with the lack of reader-curiosity inspired by an opening line such as this: 'Jane carefully knotted the ends of her scarf under her chin as she looked out of the door at the rainy afternoon'.

Of course, what follows needs to be of equal weight. Ondaatje, in *The English Patient*, offers us these lines towards the bottom of the first page: 'Every four days she washes his black body, beginning at the destroyed feet. She wets a washcloth and holding it above his ankles squeezes the water onto him . . . Above the shins the burns are worst. Beyond purple. Bone'. It is impossible not to turn the page. So the primary question is: have you hooked your readers sufficiently to ensure that they turn the first page, and keep turning till the end?

Middles

Writing a first novel is a fearsome task. If you're lucky and dedicated, and you've been planning this book for years, you may storm through it with few hitches. It's more likely, though, that you'll stumble from time to time, get stuck occasionally or even frequently, and fall into despondency and despair – if only temporarily – for the duration of the writing of the first draft.

For many writers, the honeymoon period lasts for the first three or four chapters; others get as far as the halfway mark or beyond. This is often the point at which the novelty is wearing thin and the end still seems a long way off. How do you prevent the middle from going soggy?

The middle is about developing the action, deepening the characterization, increasing the intrigue, adding complexity to the plot. You are building the structure for which you have laid the foundations, and like most other processes sandwiched between two events (in this case the opening and the closing of a story) some of the work may feel repetitive, some of it is just hard slog. However, if it is hard work to you the writer, it will also be hard work to the reader. The balance here is to maintain interest and suspense without over-complicating the main plot with too many side-issues, or losing sight of the thrust of the story.

The main function of the middle is to maintain the building of tension to the climax, which does not come, as one might suppose, actually in the middle, but close to the end. It's here that the inexorability of fate, destiny, karma, the outcome of past choices or the 'fatal flaw' of the main character (depending on your outlook) starts to kick in and make itself felt. These are the 'effects' of the opening and succeeding 'causes'. In a way things are now accelerating, even though you as writer may feel as though you are wading through mud. Your character(s) will probably have lived through an opening crisis; the middle often presents another one, the outcome of which is linked to the final crisis which forms the climax of the book.

You might want to introduce a new character or situation or an unexpected development – each of these can inject fresh vitality into a story. At this point, too, you may want to explore and develop any sub-plots that you have constructed — but as a beginning novelist it's easier to keep these to a minimum.

Perhaps here you will wish to focus on the results of some of the earlier actions of your main characters. It helps to ask questions: Why? What if? What's the worst scenario that could happen as a result of X? What could happen if character A did such and such and character B responded in this way? Or responded in that way? What could go wrong? Who would suffer most? What might happen from there? And keep asking the questions until your answers begin to be both original and startling.

Keep in mind that tension is generated as a result of the protagonist being thwarted in his or her aims and wishes by one or more antagonists (external or internal). The dynamic force of the plot hinges on cause and effect, actions and reactions.

Remember all the time that you are building towards the main crisis of the book, dropping clues, offering twists and weaving in loose strands so that the climax, and the end, when they come, can be seen to be the only possible conclusions to the events already set in motion.

The climax

The climax is the summit of the book. In retrospect it can be seen that all the action of the story has led to this moment.

At the climax, the string of the story is strung as taut as it can take – sometimes so taut that all it can do is break. A climax is usually the major crisis of the book, and often involves either suffering or the knowledge that there is a choice or decision to be made or an event to be met which will probably involve suffering. If the writer has done a good job, the reader is drawn into the intensity of the situation to the extent that he or she suffers with the characters involved. At this point, jeopardy, discovery, sacrifice and risk are key words. As in the archetypal myths from which so many of our stories continue to grow, the hero or heroine undergoes an ordeal which will change the course of his or her life for ever. A climax involves transformation.

How not to write an anticlimax

It's been said often enough, one would think; but I'll say it again. *When you get to the end, STOP.* The end is basically pretty soon after the climax, the major crisis – a few pages, maybe a (short) chapter or two. Preferably not more. Having delivered your *pièce de résistance*, don't dilute it or disappoint or insult your reader by explaining the crisis at length or exploring 'life after climax'. You will, of course, need some time to show or at least hint at the effects of the climax on the main characters; but if you've done your groundwork this should not take too long. There may be a final twist at the end – however, your reader should not be left feeling cheated, duped or patronized (for instance, with an ending such as 'and then I awoke and realized it was all a dream'; a contrived ending; or the kind of ending where it's obvious that the narrator had previously withheld a crucial piece of information).

The ending needs to offer resolution. This does not mean that all the loose ends need to be tied up – life isn't like that, either – but the major problems need to be solved or answered. Endings do not need to be happy – nor do they have to be examples of grim black 'realism'. What is important is that they are satisfying and appropriate – that the story leaves us wanting more, whilst still recognizing that it's complete. If the ending is surprising, an unanticipated shock, so much the better, as long as it fits the plot. Is it better to leave a glimmer of hope? Maybe – even if the glimmer only consists of a single survivor's determined stagger into the bleakness of a post-holocaust landscape. Perhaps as we approach a new millennium the capacity of the human spirit to endure in the face of all odds is something to be celebrated; something we all want to hear.

We want to get to the end of a book feeling changed, somehow. An ending that moves you – whether to despair, joy, laughter or anger – is an ending that has worked. An ending which leaves you feeling untouched, mildly frustrated, let down or uncomprehending is an anti-climax.

Writing practice

Opening sentences

Write ten unconnected opening sentences for imaginary stories. Each of these is to be on a different theme picked at random (not connected with your novel). Your intention is to seduce an imagined reader into wanting to know more. Here are some examples:

- That year, the ground was frozen so hard we couldn't bury the goat.
- With a wave of nausea that threatened – mercifully perhaps – to blind him, Dino realized that the ground was accelerating to meet him faster than he could hope to think of an avoidance strategy.
- It wasn't until twenty years later, standing at the open graveside, that Anna allowed herself to realize that she'd married the wrong man.
- He'd always thought Jon was joking about the man-eating monkeys in the Amazon basin – until tonight.
- At the time, a hot-air balloon accidentally landing in the front garden seemed an auspicious sign for the journey on which I was about to embark.

And now write ten possible opening sentences for your novel, whether or not you've already chosen an opening sentence. This time, of course, the theme will not be randomly chosen but quite specific. Which of these has the most power? Which is the most original? Which sums up best the tone of your opening chapter? Once again, without being too contrived, choose a sentence which has impact and drama implicit in its language.

Chapter outlines

We looked at writing chapter outlines in chapter two. Now is the time to complete this, if you haven't already.

Note down, first of all, how you're going to open the book; what the climax will be, and what the end will be (remember this is just a provisional plan). Jot down, too, other key events; each of these might make a chapter. Assuming you have a rough idea of the length of the book – say between 60,000 and 80,000 words – let's work on the basis of twelve chapters (chapters, of course, can be any length). Each chapter, therefore, will contain between 5,000 and 7,000 words approximately. (If you're not sure what this looks like, this chapter is around 4,000 words. A page of A4 typescript will contain about 500–700 words, depending on font size.)

Keep a record of these chapters as already described in chapter two.

Synopsis

Your synopsis will be based on the main events as outlined in your chapter breakdowns, though in a more fluid, seamless form. It's worth doing this for your own clarity, and you'll need it to approach publishers. Aim for around 1,000–5,000 words.

Connecting the crises

In a few sentences, note down the connection between the major crisis, or climax, of the book, and the character's central problem. The problem defines the theme of the book (and is usually, directly or indirectly, the cause of the crisis); the climax shows the inevitable crisis associated with intensifying the effects of the problem.

Ending

Finally, note down the content of the last page of your book. You might want to sketch out a draft ending.

9   Bringing the Threads Together

Pace

We looked in chapter eight at interspersing narration with scenes. Pace is to do with this balance.

There is a dynamic which comes into play in a successful book, which an author with a natural feel for language and an instinct for storytelling develops intuitively. If you are unsure about how you handle this, there are things which you might wish to bear in mind.

Narrative tension can be created, sustained and exploited in a number of ways. Some of the more obvious devices include 'hooks' to keep a reader turning the pages (for instance, if we know that Helen is desperate to avoid seeing Robert, introducing his imminent arrival will offer a hook), and 'cliffhangers' where the protagonists are left at the end of a chapter in a situation of danger, risk or crisis. Often the next chapter, in the case of the latter, will take up the story from a different place, or use flashback to keep us guessing. Perhaps a sub-plot will be introduced, or a new character, to add spice or new interest to a story. Perhaps an author will lay a false track, or several tracks.

All these, if used with care, will add to the pacing in a book. As always, however, you need to be aware of the possibilities of irritating and frustrating a reader, with the result of alienation.

Pace also includes an awareness of mood and atmosphere in a

story. The main thing to be conscious of is the need for variety, breaking up the narration in different ways: alternate periods of action with lulls, use dialogue, consider devices such as letters and diary extracts to sustain interest. Watch out, though, for any tendency to overdo it, which will only give a disjointed effect.

Scene or narrative?

The pace of a plot is determined largely by the balance of narrative versus scene-setting. Integral to scenes is dialogue, which is a further determinant of pace.

Scenes are the foundation of a book, the vehicle for the plot. They carry the action. Narration, or exposition, gives us the background: the essential information, the setting, the context, the history without which our scenes would be too intense, too claustrophobic and two-dimensional. Narration gives us explanations, fills in gaps. Inevitably, it slows up the pace, and can be used to great effect as a necessary counterpoint to the action which develops the story. Its strength (and its danger) is that it's easier to write than action scenes, and can be much briefer – in narration you can sum up what happened in a sentence or two, while the relevant scene or exposition might take several pages. Whilst you need both, scenes are arguably more important; it is the scenes which carry us through the crises and up to the major climax.

It seems to be a general truth that most novels have three major crises or turning points, the most significant one being the crisis at the climax of the book, on which rests the final outcome. Whilst there will be many more scenes than this in a book, these three dramatic ones are interrelated in that they are the major peaks in the mountain range created by the scenes. These significant turning points are called set-pieces, and it helps in terms of pace to be mindful of what these set-pieces are, where they come in the text, and how you're going to build up to them. They will have all the more impact – as do all scenes – if in juxtaposition you use a slower pace in gentle narration to throw them into relief.

Scenes, as I have already explained, consist of action portrayed as if it were unfolding in front of your eyes on a stage, *showing* the readers what happened (even if you're writing in the past tense) as it happened, rather than telling them about it from a distance.

Style

Style is connected with pace, in that it acts as a vehicle.

One important consideration is the narrative 'voice'. Whatever viewpoint you choose to take, your own authorial voice should not intrude, unless you are deliberately introducing such an intrusion for effect. Narrator's 'asides' can work of course if you are using a first-person viewpoint, and occasionally an author can get away with commenting on the story ('The gods play their own games with mankind. Rupert would never know what happened to him that day') if he or she is taking an omniscient third-person viewpoint. On the whole, though, a novel works best, and holds our attention most effectively, if we are not made to distance ourselves by an author's intrusions. You can't go far wrong if you keep your writing style smooth, flowing and unobtrusive.

With a first novel, it's easy to over-write. Too many words, and words that are unnecessarily long and complicated, can get in the way and hold up the plot. Economy of style can be beautiful; there is no need to look for the 'prettiest' way to express something if a simpler way presents itself (and flowery language can be very offputting if it's inappropriately placed).

Almost all authors benefit from reminding themselves of the maxim 'less is more'. Things to look for are too many 'he said's and 'she said's; repetition in general; over-long sentences which may lose a reader; and words which send an audience scurrying for the dictionary every few sentences. One or two are fine; nobody minds being challenged, and learning, if the story holds their attention.

Reading your work out loud, perhaps into a tape-recorder, can help you see what needs pruning, what's superfluous, which sentences are so long that you run out of breath.

You can use style to your advantage; dramatic scenes of suspense require short sentences and sharp or hard sounds; relaxed scenes, love scenes, gentle settings need longer sentences, flowing language, softer, longer words. (This usually comes naturally to writers, provided they have, as most writers do, a keen sense of observation.)

Each word should work for its living, almost as much in prose as in poetry. Nouns present no problem. Adjectives (for those of you for whom grammatical rules are a faint and shaky memory) describe and qualify a noun: a *balmy* day, a *sleek, chestnut* horse, a *sturdy oak* table, a *fleet-footed* athlete. Those of you with sharp eyes will have spotted my deliberate mistake – the tautology in the last phrase. An athlete by definition is fleet-footed, so the qualifying adjective is superfluous. The message, once again, is to use adjectives with care. One or two well-chosen ones may help a noun ignite into three dimensions; weak adjectives or too many of them will have the opposite effect. Having said that, it is said that Iris Murdoch once used sixteen successive adjectives successfully (though I've never tracked down the passage), but, unless you're Iris Murdoch, I'd be chary of doing that too often.

The same applies to adverbs: those words, often ending in 'ly', which qualify a verb. 'Successfully' in the sentence about Iris Murdoch qualified my verb 'used'. Aspiring novelists attempting to acquire a literary style can easily fall into the trap of over-liberality with both adjectives and adverbs.

Better by far is to pay attention to the real building blocks of language: the verbs. Verbs are dynamite – active, dynamic creatures. The right choice of verb, in its right form, can transform a passage. 'He walked towards her.' What a missed opportunity for characterization, for conveying mood! *How* did he walk towards her? Did he stride, amble, plod, stumble, slope, shuffle, edge, limp, lope, race, slouch, gallop, tiptoe? And which is the stronger of these two sentences?

- I was standing there with my mouth open, realizing that he was aiming my car straight for the lorry, which he was about to hit. I held my breath, waiting for the bang.
- I stood helpless, transfixed with horror, as he smashed my car into the tailgate of the stationary lorry.

You will see how the mood has changed in the second sentence, which in its sparseness of language and choice of verb and verb form ('stood transfixed', 'smashed') gives us a more direct picture of the incident than the more rambling language and verb forms of the first.

As always, you can overdose. Go for balance. The verbs chosen should not appear contrived: in a long passage of dialogue, for instance, the best option by far is to have developed your characters' voices and set the scene to the extent that you can dispense to a degree with 'he said'. But the second best option may be to repeat the 'he/she saids' if otherwise the only choice is a string of carefully researched verbs which read like a thesaurus: 'she countered', 'he responded', 'she enquired', 'he offered', 'he replied', 'she continued', 'she volunteered'. Too many of these will be more intrusive than the 'he/she saids', which at least we can overlook because they are so commonplace.

Actions speak louder than words

Or do they? Yes, if by actions we mean a dramatic scene portrayed, as opposed to the narrator's words recounting it as history. *But* most effective of all, perhaps, are the words spoken by the characters themselves.

I've said that the most frequent mistake made by beginning novelists is telling rather than showing; narration rather than portrayal. The second most common weakness in a beginner's novel is connected with this: we are told what was said as reported speech, so that even the dialogue is secondhand, and the scenes are static.

'Richard told her he didn't love her any more; in fact, that there was someone else. Susie, once she'd recovered her breath, replied shakily that she'd suspected as much for a very long time.' These two sentences might form a critical turning point in your book; but recounted like this, a reader probably won't even notice them. Make a scene of it involving dialogue, and the picture comes into focus:

Susie knew something was up the minute Richard came into the room. She could sense a certain gritted determination about him; and besides, his tie was askew and his hair looked as if he'd been running his hands through it all afternoon. She felt very still, suddenly, very frightened. She hardly dared breathe.

Richard sat down heavily, and removed his glasses. Always a bad sign.

They both spoke at once. She heard her own voice, high and tinny:

'What's up?'

Richard didn't look at her. 'I don't know how to say this, Sooz. It's . . . I'm . . . You know we've always said we'll be honest with each other . . .'

The moment hung. Susie swallowed, heard him clear his throat. She didn't dare speak. Her knees felt weak, all of a sudden. She sat down herself, carefully folding her skirt around her legs.

'Susan.'

He never called her Susan. This was serious.

'I think we need to talk.'

Susie felt an urgent rush of irritation, anger, underneath her fear. How tired she was, suddenly, of all this dissembling. 'For goodness' sake, Richard, get on with it. Just *tell* me!' She suddenly knew, with a moment's appalling piercing clarity, what he was going to say. 'The phone calls. The late nights. The business conferences. There's someone else, isn't there?' She heard her voice shake, but she'd said it; and as she did, she realized she'd known all the time. A cold fury crept over her; her hands felt

146

clammy. She clenched them in her lap, willed herself not to shake.

'I've realized I . . . I . . . don't love you any more. At least, I do –
but not enough. Not in the right—'

She didn't let him finish. All the hurt, all the anger, all the frus-
tration of the last decade, with all its lies, welled up in her, and she
was on her feet in an instant, and in one fluid motion she'd
wrenched the brass standard lamp away from its socket and
launched herself at him. For a fraction of a moment she was a
Valkyrie, a Boadicea, a raging warrior . . .

Nothing will bring a book, a character, a scene alive as much as
dialogue; and, not surprisingly, many new writers shy away from it.
Yes, it is demanding. Dialogue carries great weight; much of our
sympathy or otherwise for a character is determined by what she
or he says – or doesn't say. Much characterization is carried by
dialogue. To create a number of different voices, stick with and
sustain them, and enable us to hear the plot through them, is difficult; all the more so since the speech needs to appear natural and
uncontrived, while still being censored by the author for the banal
trivialities which make up much of our 'real-life' day-to-day
conversation.

Creating exciting, credible dialogue

Dialogue, then, can be used to show us character; to carry the
story; to convey thoughts, emotions, dreams and aspirations – in
short, the inner life of our characters; to give us necessary history
and background in a dramatic and succinct way; to introduce,
heighten or sustain conflict and tension; to set a scene; to portray
relationships; to convey something of the age, social standing and
lifestyle of characters, and to engage the reader.

Dialogue is the number one opportunity, the primary tool, for
a novelist to show us who someone is; through it, characters
reveal themselves, their fears and dreams, their conflicts, what is

important to them. We learn more about people, their attitudes and responses, through their conversation than through anything else.

The cardinal sin for a novelist, as Victor Pritchett was quoted as saying in chapter seven, is to have your characters reading one another's minds through the author. Almost as ineffective is to have your characters speaking directly to the reader, as if to a camera. They need to communicate directly with each other, relate to each other, live with, love or hate each other. Dialogue is intimately linked with characterization inasmuch as the vocabulary chosen, the thoughts expressed and the way of expressing them must be consistent with the character speaking. This is where a detailed character portrait can be invaluable.

There's no substitute for eavesdropping. Catch any snippet of interesting conversation you hear anywhere in your notebook – you never know when it might come in useful. Treat yourself to an hour or two in a lively café, and – discreetly – tune in to the conversations around you. Do they match the appearance of the speakers? What might you learn about their characters, homes and lifestyles from the snippets of dialogue? How do people really speak? How much of what they say is 'padding', and would need to be edited if it occurred in a work of fiction? How much of the trivial mundanities might you choose to include in order to avoid your conversations seeming contrived or clinical? Listen to live shows on the radio, where to some extent the participants are editing or censoring themselves. I'm not sure this is a morally acceptable suggestion, but a tape-recorder might be a useful item; if not to take out to a café, then to switch on at home (be aware of the possibility of divorce petitions if you make a habit of this!), or at least into which you might read your created conversations. Playing them back will enable you to spot weaknesses more easily than you might on paper.

A word of warning: long passages of unbroken dialogue can be just as wearing (as well as confusing) for a reader as long passages of narrative. You can break them up with action, which will also serve to remind us of background and setting. Let's backtrack to a previous scene in the life of Richard and Susie:

'I'm just bloody sick of it all, all this –' Richard waved his arms at the mass of papers on the floor – 'you just seem to have no respect for my needs. You know I hate mess.' He swooped angrily on the nearest bundle of papers and flung them towards the rubbish bin. The cats scattered. 'That's it. I've had enough.'

She could hear his heavy breathing. She took a deep breath and opened her mouth to retaliate, protest, apologize, she didn't know which, but already he was gone, slamming the door behind him. Another late night at the office now, no doubt. 'Oh God,' she groaned, slumping down into the heap of papers overflowing the sofa. 'Oh God, oh God, oh God.'

This brings us to the question of swearing and blasphemy. This is one of those grey areas, which really is down to personal preferences, and style. For all writers there comes a time when risk-taking is what will bring their writing alive, and unless each of your characters is a clone of yourself, you will be writing 'out of character' for a great deal of your time. If your character is the kind of person who would swear or blaspheme, then there's no way out of it. As always, it's a question of balance. Where the odd swear-word will have impact, a diet of them will dilute a piece of writing.

Slang is another tricky area. If you use it, get it right; remember how important it is in terms of dating and typecasting your character and his or her era. A 1950s colonel is unlikely to say 'cool' or 'groovy'. A street kid from Brooklyn is not going to speak grammatically perfect Radio 4 English with full glottal stops.

Accents deserve a mention. They are hard to convey on paper, at least without falling into stereotypes and/or driving a reader up the wall. Better to convey ethnic origins or foreign nationality with the odd well-chosen phrase, or perhaps with the occasional inversion of the natural word order such as a non-native speaker might use.

What is the key ingredient for fresh, living, sparkling dialogue? I think there are two. One is being able so to identify with your characters that you live the scene and its conversation as you write it. Think yourself into their rôles, their backgrounds, their language. Picture yourself in their body, their clothes, their chair. How does the scene in which they're participating make them feel? If you struggle with this, you could try making notes about the setting and associated emotions before you write the dialogue. Is so-and-so shy, inhibited, uncomfortable with confrontation? Or is he passionate by nature? Is she an extrovert who loves a good fight? How would this reflect on their words, their postures and actions, or their physical response to the situation? How would they deliver whatever they would say in this context?

The second is letting go of your normal writing style and any preconceived ideas about what you should and shouldn't say, what is and what isn't good grammar, in order to allow the flow of what people say in such a situation – what *these* people would say in *this* situation – to dictate the writing. Most of us speak in a far less formal way than we would write, or than our education has suggested that we should. Interestingly, it's often far harder for well-educated people to write good dialogue; they seem to find it more difficult to let go of ideas surrounding the correct way to express something. Their dialogue tends to be peppered with subjunctives, perfectly ordered clauses and neatly finished sentences, which is just not how most people speak in real life, no matter how well educated; or at least not in moments of conflict or passion.

Perhaps there's a third ingredient: choosing which passages to convey in dialogue. Many of these will coincide with the parts of the story out of which you've chosen to make scenes: anywhere where tension, conflict or passion are being enacted.

Try out the alternatives. Dialogue is powerful. Writing a scene in dialogue, even if later you change it to narrative, will bring it alive for you in a way that little else can.

Writing practice

Creating a life for your characters

Your character is about to wake up. Spend fifteen minutes or so recording in writing his or her start to a typical (or atypical) day. Record the character's first thoughts and feelings, first impressions on waking, the first things he or she does, the people, animals or objects he or she sees. What is the character's waking environment? What are his or her routines? What thoughts are running through his or her mind in the shower? At breakfast? What does he or she eat for breakfast? And how – standing up, reading the paper, holding a conversation? Is this person a morning or evening person? Does he or she like or loathe conversation first thing?

Now consider how your character reacts under stress. Have him or her open a piece of mail containing bad news at breakfast. Write a paragraph describing his or her reactions and ensuing actions. (The aim of both these pieces is to further acquaint yourself with your character and his or her environment.)

Would the above paragraph make a good opening scene for a book or a chapter? If so, how would you rewrite it for maximum possible impact?

Creating a scene through visualization

The most effective way of working with this is to read it into a tape-recorder, allowing the necessary pauses. Or ask a friend to read you through it.

Close your eyes.

You find yourself in front of a door. (Pause.)

In a minute, you are going to open it, and you know that the other side of that door you will find some of the characters from your book, acting out a scene in front of you. Give yourself a minute to try and picture which scene this will be. (Pause.)

When you're ready, open the door and step through into that scene as if you are either the main character or a witness looking on.

What's the first thing that you hear?

What else? (Pause to record this.)

Close your eyes again.

Any particular smells? Look around you. What can you see? (Make notes if necessary.)

What are the predominant colours?

If there are people involved, note the clothes they wear, the expressions on their faces and their physical postures and/or gestures. (Pause to make notes.)

What's your general impression of the scene in which you find yourself? What's the mood? How does it make you feel?

When you have seen enough, step back out of the scene and close the door.

When you're ready, open your eyes and write the scene, drawing on your notes and remembering the rôle of the five senses in creating credible scenes. Does the scene you have witnessed remind you of any event in your own life? If so, draw on your memories of this for impact.

Include dialogue in your scene if possible.

Creating dialogue

Imagine a scene which involves a conflict, confrontation or misunderstanding. There should be at least two people involved. This can be simple, such as returning an unwanted item to a store, or it can involve a potentially funny element, such as a case of mistaken identity.

Write out the whole scene in dialogue. Can you encapsulate the different characters in their responses/relationship to each other and the situation? Remember that a conflict between strangers will use different language from that between lovers, or a parent and a wayward teenager, or sworn enemies.

10   Developing Your Work

Overwriting

One of the most difficult things for a writer, and especially a novelist, is learning to let go of a piece of work. Once it's 'out there' in the big wide world fending for itself on – hopefully – a few booksellers' shelves, one's feelings towards it change somewhat; often these are a mixture of immense pride coupled with that kind of retrospective wisdom that enables you to see all its shortcomings.

Before you get to that point, however, you're likely to go through all the umbilical struggles that any parent will recognize. It's the literary equivalent of sending a child to school for the first time – you're forever tugging at her socks, wiping his snotty nose, straightening ties/hair ribbons/shoelaces. (Though there are, of course, a minority of writers who, convinced that what they've written is the most astonishing act of creativity since the pyramids, can't wait to lob it at some poor unsuspecting publisher's desk the minute they've penned the last word.)

Your work will clearly need some reworking, some editing – of which more later. But in the need to make it perfect, many authors fall into the trap of overworking it, writing and rewriting it until it bears little resemblance to the original. Separation anxiety? Fear of failure? Fear of success? All of these, perhaps, and other things. This can, of course, strengthen a work, but it's not always so. It's easy to lose the power of the original thought or idea by overwriting it; so easy to rub the sheen off its wings. All creative writing tutors will have had the experience of watching an inspired piece of writing die slowly as its creator worries it, teases it, batters it into shape. This seems especially to happen at the end of a book, where the original climax and resolution is gradually diluted as it is written and rewritten; it has something to do with the writer's reluctance to acknowledge that the book is now finished and must go.

Overwriting involves the 'trying too hard' which usually accompanies a beginner's enthusiasm in her or his attempt to learn the art. You may notice as you reread your book that gradually and subtly your style changes as you think yourself into the plot, feel yourself into the life of the characters. The more absorbed you are in what you're writing, the less likely you are to be forcing the writing, and slowly your own natural style will appear as you relax into the confidence that comes with the act of creating something. Passages which read as stilted, contrived or pretentious tend to occur more towards the beginning of a book on the whole. So what can be learnt from this? Perhaps the key is not to force your writing; to look for the most economic and exact way of expressing your ideas, whilst still allowing the flow and inspiration which will lift your writing out of the purely pedestrian. A reader, then, is less likely to be aware of you as author, which can only be a good thing – unless you're using this for effect, which takes experience, skill and, usually, fame.

Pruning

One of the problems with a first novel is that the temptation is to cram all one's stories, all one's philosophies, all one's experiences, all one's best love scenes, fantasies, gory details, knowledge, and descriptions into one book, regardless of whether they fit or not. The result of this can be, sadly, either a shambolic mess or a plot that is tweaked and jammed and dismembered and stretched in a Procrustean effort to fit it around the 'inspired passages'.

You need to be able to train your eye to spot the difference between a piece of vibrant, spontaneous writing which flames into life off the page with no reworking, and writing which masquerades under the mantle of spontaneous genius but actually rambles, unstructured, overwritten and pointless, into nowhere.

Seasoned novelists will tell you that, at final draft stage, the scenes which had seemed the most successful, the most lyrical, the most inspired, were often the very ones that had to go. Keep your eyes on the alert for those beautifully written passages of which you were so proud. Do they contribute to the plot? Do they move the story forward, fill in vital information, create a background or context? Do they serve the book, or are they there to show the world how well you write? (I know; I'm guilty of it myself.) If a piece needs reworking in order to make the syntax work, or to preserve some beauty and present it in a less over-the-top fashion, fine. But consider the possibility of cutting it altogether, particularly if it's superfluous or irrelevant. Peter Sansom once said (speaking of poetry) that too often a writer was content with merely straightening a poem's tie, when actually it needed a whole new suit of clothes. The same thing could be applied to prose. Keep a record of these 'inspired' pieces, by all means; start another book!

It's been said that most novels benefit from being cut by a third. If this would mean that your word count fell below, say, 45,000, it may be worth reconsidering the plot. Is it a bit insubstantial, thin? Resist the temptation to use 'padding' to compensate.

While we're on length, what should you aim for? It's unlikely that a first novel of over 150,000 words would be considered – the bigger the book, the higher the costs of production. You need to prove yourself first. (An exception to this might be the first volume of an exciting saga with potential mass appeal, or which offers film or TV possibilities.) If it drops below 50,000 it will need to be a good strong story where every word counts. If you aim for 60,000–80,000 you won't be too far adrift.

But go carefully with your pruning knife. By all means rework sentences for clarity and/or brevity, if otherwise they get in the way of the story, but try and bring to your work the delicacy of a masseur's touch as well as a surgeon's scalpel.

Editing and revising

It's unlikely that your finished novel will be perfect in its first draft form. This is especially true for those novelists who write their books in chunks, constructing scenes first and only later linking them all together.

In order to be able to assess and edit your work successfully, you need to be able to bring a degree of objectivity to it; this means putting it away for weeks, if not months, in order to gain some distance and perspective on it. The best thing you can do is to start writing a new book!

If you're the kind of writer who tends to edit as you go, revising the previous day's work before starting the next day's, you will have a reasonably good idea of the book's shape, and may have fewer surprises. If you've slung it all together and haven't really looked back, you may be astonished at what you've written from the perspective of three months later – whether at the paucity or the richness.

Here are some guidelines for editing (some recap points already made).

Read your work out loud: to yourself, to someone else, into a tape-recorder. Listen for clumsy phraseology, unclear syntax and repetition and unnecessary padding.

Look out, too, for the 'boredom factor' – unless what your hero is eating for breakfast is relevant, riveting or gives you an excuse to show off your exceptional sensory descriptive skills, do we really need a page of it? It may be, on the other hand, that your particular strength is turning everyday scenes such as meals into a story; after all Peter Mayle did this with *A Year in Provence*, which became a best-seller, so it can be done. You may need objective opinions on this.

Be ruthless about pruning. This includes 'little' words, clichés and extra adjectives. All writing is improved by the right adjective rather than several 'nearly' ones. The same goes for adverbs: choose a precise verb. 'He fled around the corner' has more impact than 'he ran quickly around the corner'.

If you find yourself emotionally attached to a passage, be suspicious. If it does not contribute directly to the plot, consider taking it out.

Are your sentences over-long, so that there's a risk of losing the syntax or the thread? If a sentence takes more than one breath to read out, or feedback from someone else implies that they have to read a sentence several times to get the gist of it, rewrite it.

Unless you're writing a literary novel, beware of too much abstraction. Keeping your writing grounded in the world of the five senses as much as possible brings it alive. Remember the importance of context; nothing happens in a vacuum. If you can't picture the setting for your writing, the reader certainly won't be able to.

If you're wanting to convey a particular message or philosophy, you may need to watch that you don't fall into didacticism. You may choose to characterize your individuals by their philosophy or values, of course; what can be offputting to a reader, however, is the novelist intruding with proselytizing opinions, even though someone who knows you well might be able to see your identification with one or more of the characters and their motivations, ideologies and conflicts.

It's worth taking care when putting 'real' people into your novels. Reactions can vary from huffiness to divorce and libel suits.

Learn to fabricate. If you are drawing on life experiences, remember that to hold the attention of anyone other than yourself and adoring family members, you will need to embroider the plain cloth of everyday experience unless your life has been exceptionally exciting. Remember that it's the job of the non-fiction writer to report history as it was; it's the job of the novelist to recreate it, to add colour and texture, to develop the 'what ifs'; to tell it like it wasn't, but might have been.

It's important not to patronize your readers by explaining too much. A novelist needs to credit them with enough imagination and intelligence to fill in the gaps – this is part of the fun of reading.

Remember the importance of showing rather than telling; and of dialogue.

Keep notes on each chapter, so that blue-eyed Lucy hasn't metamorphosed into brown-eyed Hannah by chapter ten. As writer you need to keep in mind, also, the passing years and correct ages of the characters throughout the book. These are simple, seemingly obvious details, and yet so often forgotten.

Punctuation and spelling clearly need checking. A spellcheck on a computer or word processor isn't infallible; it won't distinguish misspelling if the word exists in another form too, e.g. borough/burrow, principle/principal. It's worth investing in a good dictionary and a book on grammar, such as *Fowler's Modern English Usage* or Michael Legat's *Nuts and Bolts of Writing*.

Finally, setting your book in a particular place requires that you ensure that all the facts relating to that place are correct.

Editorial help

It seems to me that objective, impartial feedback and advice on a novel is invaluable. It's hard, sadly, for family members and close friends to look critically and constructively at your book. Either they'll think it's wonderful because they love you and in any case wouldn't want to hurt your feelings, or they'll be over-judgemental because they want to help you as much as they can (or for reasons of their own, such as jealousy).

If there is someone whose literary intelligence, objectivity and integrity you respect and trust, their opinions are worth their weight in gold (to use a cliché). Perhaps I could just make a plea, though, on behalf of all those successful but harassed authors who receive a number of requests (often accompanied by full manuscripts) from strangers, along the lines of: 'I know this is a bit cheeky, but I'm a great fan of your work. Would you mind just casting your eyes over this novel of mine and tell me what you think?' Yes, it is a bit cheeky. It also involves several days' work, for which you'd pay a three-figure sum through the official channels.

So failing the perfect literary friend, the very best thing you can do is to avail yourself of the services of an editorial consultant. In a market so very small, with the number of unsolicited manuscripts so very huge, you could be increasing your chances of publication significantly.

An editorial consultant is not the same thing as a literary agent. An agent – almost as hard to find as a publisher – is concerned with finding a publisher for your book. Some of them charge a nominal reading fee; all of them charge a commission on royalties.

An editorial consultant offers advice and assessment of your work, for a fee. He or she will normally have a background in writing, publishing and editing. What they offer is an appraisal service and written report, exploring in some detail such things as characterization, dialogue, plot and writing style. Knowing the market as they do (or certainly should) they will have an insight both into the book's strengths and weaknesses, and into what market the book might or might not fit. They will make suggestions as to what needs changing.

Some of them will offer a proofreading and copy-editing service, sometimes as part of the main appraisal, sometimes as a separate service. If you're not worried about the actual story but know that your grammar, spelling or presentation might be weak, then I can't emphasize enough how important it is to get this right – or as right as possible. It's true that a publisher *may* overlook shaky spelling and poor grammar if the story is exciting and original enough, but it is, as they say, a buyer's market with literally thousands of unsolicited manuscripts landing on publishers' desks each week or even each day. This means that only the ones that are outstanding in every way are likely to get consideration – that is, to have more than the letter and first paragraph scanned. Since the ending of the Net Book Agreement, and with the advent of videos and the internet, the publishing industry has had a difficult time of it, and not all houses can still afford to pay in-house or external readers to plough through every submission.

Editorial consultants advertise in the classified sections of magazines such as *Writers' News, Writing Magazine* and *The New Writer.*

Presentation and submission

With the publishing market as difficult as it is to break into, presentation is all important. We've talked about grammar and spelling. Presentation clearly includes what your manuscript actually looks like. There are a number of books available which go into this aspect in some detail, so we'll just skim through it.

Your manuscript should be on white paper and clean – no coffee rings. Each page should be numbered, titled and with your name on it. No fancy paper, fancy bindings, scented offerings, coloured inks. And absolutely no handwritten manuscripts – sorry, they won't even be looked at. The script should be double-spaced: this means a line of space inserted automatically between every line of text. New paragraphs should be indented, but the line-spacing before and after each paragraph should *not* be increased. A cover sheet with the title of the work, your name, address and approximate word-count (rounded up to the nearest thousand), should be included.

The submission normally consists of a synopsis and three chapters. Opinion is divided on whether these should be consecutive opening chapters, or three at random. You will need to enclose a stamped, addressed envelope with the appropriate postage. Send your offering loose-leaf, with just a retaining rubber band or in a simple card folder, in a sturdy envelope or bag.

Synopses, you will remember, function as the story in brief. You'll be drawing on the chapter outlines which you've kept in a separate section of your folder. These should record, in note form, the main events of each chapter. If you write them out as a summation of the story, linking the incidents smoothly, you should then have your synopsis. Somewhere between 1,000 and 5,000 words is common.

Publishers like to know what the ending is going to be. On the whole, it's best not to keep them guessing; it won't encourage them to ask for the whole manuscript, they're more likely to assume that you don't know how to end your book. In addition, they prefer it if you have an idea what category your book will fit into. This is not easy if your book is of the 'contemporary' kind which tends more to character-driven than plot-driven stories, and draws on a number of areas. If, however, you can outline its substance in a sentence, you'll have an advantage.

The covering letter should be polite, to the point and not pushy. Give the publisher information relevant to the submission – if you've had anything published in a reputable journal (not simply the parish magazine), tell them. List any relevant experience or qualifications, or the fact that you're reading for your Creative Writing MA at Sussex, if you should be so lucky. That Auntie Mabel thought it was good, or that you used to do well in English at school, will not impress them. If you have nothing useful that will help your chances, don't make it up or throw in details which will mark you out as an amateur.

Should you only send your offering to one publisher at a time? This used to be a matter of etiquette; however since publishers can hang on to a manuscript for up to nine months, you could be in a nursing home by the time it's accepted. More people are sending out multiple submissions, now; perhaps it's courteous to mention to a prospective publisher if you're doing this.

How long should you wait before querying? If you haven't heard back within six weeks, a polite letter might not go amiss. If you still hear nothing, it's safe to assume that the publisher is not interested.

Don't be discouraged by rejection slips. It's very, very rare for a novel to be accepted first time. Some of our literary greats had their novels rejected tens, and even scores, of times. If it's good, and you're persistent, it should find a publisher eventually. Have a strategy. Make a list in advance of all the publishing houses who deal with your kind of novel (do your homework in bookshops and through *The Writer's Handbook* and *The Writers' and Artists' Yearbook*). Find out the name of the commissioning editor through the switchboard. If and when it comes back to you, send it out again immediately.

Agents

You'll find, if you ask around, that writers divide almost equally into those who wouldn't be without an agent, and those who would prefer to deal direct with a publisher themselves. There are, of course, pros and cons both ways.

An agent will: know where to send your book; carry some clout; vet and negotiate contracts; make sure you're paid. Agents also have the kind of automatic entry to a publishing house that authors often don't. This may be increasingly important, as more publishing houses specify that they will only look at work that comes to them via an agent. An agent will be putting in an enormous effort on your behalf, as your success is reflected in their income. A good agent may also be your friend.

Against this, an agent: will cost you money; may lose interest in your work if it's not selling; want to handle all your future work (assuming you're successful); be a buffer between yourself and your publisher, which isn't always a good thing, as there's nothing like personal contact to build up a relationship with your editor and publisher.

Once you have a book published, or a contract signed and sealed, you qualify for membership of the Society of Authors. I would strongly recommend joining; not only do they present a number of talks of interest to writers of all genres throughout the year, but membership allows you to send them up publishers' contracts for vetting before signing them. This in itself is a major reason for many writers to find an agent (and believe me, once you've seen a publishing contract you'll understand why this is helpful). They also act as a kind of union, defending and protecting authors' rights in a range of areas. They offer advice and publish a number of information leaflets, as well as a useful and interesting journal.

Reading and writing

I've said before that the fact that you're writing a novel is no excuse for not doing any other kind of writing. On the contrary, keeping a journal, doing writing practice or writing poetry, short stories or articles will stretch your brain and keep your creative muscles toned. Any other writing you do can only nourish and enhance the novel-writing.

There is no substitute, as I've already said, for reading, reading and more reading. It's important not just to see what's being published and what publishers and readers are looking for, but also to see how other writers tackle this writing business. Allow yourself initially at least to learn from, if not to be influenced by, others; notice what they do successfully and how they achieve it. Credit yourself, too, with the authority and skill to notice what doesn't work, and why. Never mind what the critics thought of (to pick a selection at random) Dickens, Dostoevsky or Sartre; or of Penelope Lively, A.S. Byatt, Ben Okri, Terry Pratchett, Pat Barker, Peter Carey, Jilly Cooper or Milan Kundera. What do *you* think? Why?

Passion and authenticity

The biggest favour you can do yourself is to enjoy what you're doing. The well-known creative writing tutor Brenda Ueland said: 'In your own work, whatever you love will be easy to write.'

A writer's life is both hard and immensely rewarding. There is nothing quite like completing a written work – except getting it published.

If you love and believe in what you're doing, that will be conveyed to the reader. Books – words – *do* change lives. They have immense power. To be in a position to communicate something about which you feel passionate is a tremendous privilege, and maybe also a responsibility. To create a world in which a reader may lose (or find) him- or herself for the duration of your story, to shed light on a small aspect of 'the human condition', to create a modern fairy story, to show what the human spirit can survive – and still come up smiling, to show how it is, to show how it could be, to describe how it was and how it might have been, to amuse, to uplift, to inspire, to allow us to feel, to teach, to offer insight and understanding, to enchant, to make relationships, to illustrate similarities, to demonstrate differences, to alleviate loneliness, to build bridges – books do all these things, and more. To be able to enthuse someone else for your story, with your language, is a gift.

How far does one compromise for one's 'art'? While one of the advantages of being an author is the ability to explore and experiment with a number of voices and styles, the best writing, I believe, is born from a passionate involvement with one's subject. You need to believe in your story, care about your characters, explore what it means to be human through the drama that is a novel. If you're in it just 'for the money', then you'd be better going and selling insurance. You need a commitment to your book. Believe in it; live it in your imagination as you write it.

And when you've finished, start another.

Support

Writing, as I said in the beginning, is a lonely business. Writers have to be to some extent introverted, or at least to cultivate the discipline of solitude. Learning to say no, as I've also already said, is a crucial part of this business. If *you* don't take yourself seriously, who will?

If you're lucky, you'll have family and friends who support you in what you do. Nonetheless, perhaps the best support a writer can have is from other writers. The stimulus of sharing the problems and the triumphs with someone who understands exactly what you're talking about, who empathizes, cannot be over-estimated.

How do you find these fellow misguided souls? Writing magazines are probably the most obvious place to start. There are a number available: either 'glossies', such as *Writing Magazine* or *Writers' News*, available from your newsagent or by subscription, or the small press literary magazines with a low circulation, again available by subscription. The bigger ones offer articles, general information, columns by experts, and details of courses, conferences, competitions, groups, editorial services and publishing news, and may include reviews and fiction or poetry. The smaller magazines largely exist to showcase short fiction and poetry. Some of them also run advertisements and reviews. The former may be found through enquiry at libraries, bookshops and newsagents. The latter are listed in a useful annually updated publication, the *Small Press Guide*, by the Writers' Bookshop in London.

There are also a number of magazines which fit in between the two categories I've mentioned; *The New Writer* is one of these.

Probably the most helpful thing you can do for yourself, at least in the early stages of writing, is to join a workshop or writers' group. Ask at your local library or adult education centre. With teaching, feedback, peer support and exchanges of ideas and information, your writing skills will develop in leaps and bounds. Week-long courses with established novelists at places like the Arvon Foundation's three centres, or Ty Newydd in Wales, will be of enormous benefit.

However, probably the maximum level of support and inspiration can be derived from groups which meet regularly, especially if you then have a deadline for producing a piece of work! The only word of caution I would offer is to choose your group carefully. If it's tutored, you will get a 'feel' for the teacher's abilities fairly quickly; if you're unsure, don't be afraid to question, and ask for credentials if necessary. The fact that a tutor has a string of published novels to his or her credit doesn't necessarily mean he or she can teach. There again, someone with a B.Ed. in English Literature may know everything there is to know about Piers Plowman and the development of the English novel from the medieval romance through to E.M. Forster, and have no idea how to construct a plot. Use your intuition.

If it's untutored, you may need to check how structured the sessions are, what the general levels of ability and professionalism may be, and whether it errs towards self-congratulation on the one hand or harsh criticism on the other. You need to come away from a group feeling that you've learnt something in the company of like-minded people who have the best interests of literature, as well as each other, at heart.

And finally

All that remains to say is: here are some guidelines. I hope they may be helpful. But when it comes down to it, you are your only authority. Only you will find the way that is right for you; all creative works are a step into uncharted territory, which is just how it should be. I wish you courage, imagination, inspiration, persistence and good writing companions along the way!

Bibliography

Dibell, A., Scott Card, O., and Turco, L., *How to Write a Mi££ion* (Robinson, 1995)

Fairfax, John and Moat, John, *The Way to Write*, (Elm Tree Books, 1981)

Forster, E.M., *Aspects of the Novel*, (Edward Arnold, 1927, Penguin, 1990)

Goldberg, Natalie, *Wild Mind*, (Rider, USA 1990, UK 1993)

Goldberg, Natalie, *Writing Down the Bones*, (Shambhala, USA 1986)

Johnson, Robert, *Inner Work*, (Harper & Row, 1989)

Legat, Michael, *The Nuts and Bolts of Writing*, (Robert Hale Ltd., 1989)

Legat, Michael, *Plotting the Novel*, (Robert Hale Ltd., 1992)

Lodge, David, *The Art of Fiction*, (Penguin, 1992)

McCallum, Chriss, *How to Write for Publication*, (How To Books, 1989)

Novakovich, Josip, *Fiction Writer's Workshop*, (Story Press USA, 1995)

Oliver, Marina, *Writing and Selling a Novel*, (How To Books, 1996)

Tobias, Ronald B., *Twenty Master Plots and How to Build Them*, (Piatkus hardback, 1995)

Small Press Guide, Writers' Bookshop (published annually)

Useful Addresses

Freelance Market News
Sevendale House
7 Dale Street
Manchester
M1 1JB

The New Writer
P.O. Box 60
Cranbrook
Kent
TN17 2ZR

QWF (Quality Women's Fiction) magazine
(also Focus on Fiction Correspondence Course)
71 Bucknill Crescent
Hamilton
Rugby
CV21 4HE

The Society of Authors
84 Drayton Road
London
SW10 9SB

Women Writers' Network Newsletter
10 Mayfield Road
London
W3 9HQ

Writer's Bulletin
P.O. Box 96
Altrincham
Cheshire
WA14 2LN

Writers' News, Writing Magazine
P.O. Box 4
Nairn
Scotland
IV12 4HU

Courses and workshops

The Arvon Foundation
Totleigh Barton
Sheepwash
Beaworthy
Devon
EX21 5NS

Also at:

Lumb Bank
Heptonstall
Hebden Bridge
W. Yorks.
HX7 6DF

and:

Moniack Mhor
Teavarran
Kiltarlity
Beauly
Inverness-shire
IV4 7HT

Fire in the Head/Flow in the Fingers
(Writing courses, editorial, visualization tapes)
P.O. Box 17
Crapstone
Yelverton
Devon
PL20 6YF

The Taliesin Trust
Ty Newydd
Llanystumdwy
Cricieth
Gwynedd
LL52 0LW

Index